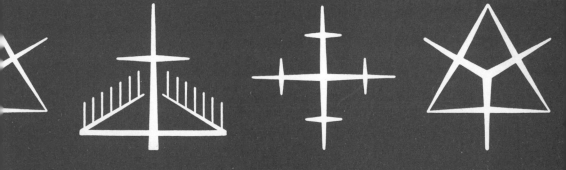

THE
UNITY
OF
THE CHURCH

THE
UNITY
OF
THE CHURCH

A Symposium

Papers Presented to the
Commissions on Theology and Liturgy
of the Lutheran World Federation

AUGUSTANA PRESS
Rock Island, Illinois

THE UNITY OF THE CHURCH

Edited by The Department of Theology
Lutheran World Federation
Geneva, Switzerland, 17 Route de Malagnou

Library of Congress Catalog Card Number 57-10288

⟦PRINTED IN U·S·A·⟧

AUGUSTANA BOOK CONCERN
Printers and Binders
ROCK ISLAND, ILLINOIS

Preface

THIS volume contains essays or lectures which were presented to the Commissions on Theology and Liturgy of the Lutheran World Federation. During the years 1954 to 1956 these Commissions studied the Unity of the Church and the Theology of Worship. The papers as now presented are simply expressions of the thinking of individual theologians and not expressions of the final result of the findings of the Commissions. These papers were essays presented and discussed in the Commissions and give a view of contemporary Lutheran thinking, its consensus as well as its tensions. The papers mostly reflect the basis on which Lutheran churches today have to start discussions in working towards a final consensus. Such agreement, however, cannot come about as the result of a few meetings but requires a continued thorough study. It can, nevertheless, be said with confidence that these beginnings have already shown evidence of an underlying consensus in the relevant principles of the Unity of the Church and of the Theology of its Worship. The papers are presented here in the hope that they will stimulate further study on these essential issues.

VILMOS VAJTA

Contents

I

The Unity of the Church

Our Oneness in Christ and Our Disunity as Churches

BY PROF. CONRAD BERGENDOFF

IT IS NOT EASY to formulate what is meant to be expressed by this theme. The committee which framed it—at Lund—debated long on its exact wording. It became apparent that no one statement would describe adequately what in reality is not a simple situation.

For example it might seem from the theme that Christians could find their unity in and with Christ without much reference to the church or churches. There are indeed some individuals who interpret Christianity as a private matter—they are Christians, they say, but they are not interested in the churches. This certainly would not be the position of those in the Faith and Order Movement. We can in fact not speak about our oneness in Christ without relating that oneness to some church in which we found Christ. The first half of the theme is not independent of the second, to be joined to it by a simple copula. It would be more accurate to say "our oneness in Christ despite our disunity as churches," or "our oneness in Christ underlying our disunity as churches."

For we cannot speak of Christ apart from the churches, nor of the churches without implying a unity that makes them a church. A church without Christ would not be a church, but any church that claims a relationship to Christ immediately finds itself related to others in Christ. "For through him we both have our access in one Spirit to the Father" (Eph. 2:18). These words were directed by Paul to such as had been alienated or separated from other of God's people but had found the wall of partition down when they came to Christ. "So then you are no more strangers and sojourners, but you are fellow citizens with the saints, and members of the household of God." Whatever be the disunity of the churches, in so far as they are churches at all they are of the household of God and their people are fellow citizens. Our oneness in Christ implies a unity of church people which cannot be obscured by any self-sufficiency of any church.

This great fact of the oneness of the church has its classic expression in Paul's imagery of the body of Christ. Even as God's purpose of redemption of mankind was effected through the incarnation by which He who existed in the form of God took the form of a servant, being found in fashion as a man (Phil. 2:8) so the believing member is incorporated into the body of Christ and lives through the power that wrought the resurrection and ascension (Eph. 1:19-23) and is the life of the church. To be in the church is to be in Christ, for life in the church is participation in the life of Christ. To stand outside the church is to remain in the family whose head is Adam and whose nature is sin and death and judgment. To have been adopted into the new creation whose head is Christ is to "receive the abundance of grace and the gift of righteousness" which reign in the life He inaugurates (Rom. 5:17).

From this point of view Christ cannot be divided (1 Cor. 1:13). "For as the body is one, and hath many members, and all the members of the body, being many, are one body, so also is Christ. For in one Spirit we were all baptized into one body—whether Jews or Greeks, whether bond or free—and were all made to drink of one Spirit" (1 Cor. 12:12-13). When we look to Christ, the head, we see only one body, the people who are His through His work and who acknowledge Him as their Lord and Savior. Our oneness in Christ is the unity of Christ with His people and of His members with one another. We are related to other Christians not directly but via the head, Christ. The other branches on the vine are in Him and therefore joined with us. We do not establish a relationship with them. He establishes us in a relationship with each other. We may or may not recognize the relationship, but this does not make or unmake a fact which He has created.

Luther exactly portrays this Pauline conception of our oneness in Christ as the oneness of the church in his words in the Large Catechism: "I believe that there is upon earth a holy assembly and congregation of pure saints, under one head, even Christ, called together by the Holy Ghost in one faith, one mind and understanding, with manifold gifts, yet one in love, without sects or schisms. And I also am a part and member of the same, a participant and joint owner of all the good it possesses, brought to it and incorporated into it by the Holy Ghost, in that I have heard and continue to hear the Word of God, which is the means of entrance. For formerly, before we had attained to this, we were of the devil, knowing nothing of God and of Christ. Thus, until the last day, the Holy Ghost abides with the holy congregation or Christian people. By means of this congregation he brings us to Christ and teaches and preaches to us the Word, whereby he works and promotes sanctification, causing (this community) daily to grow and become strong in the faith and fruits of the Spirit, which he produces."

Our theme rightly places first "our oneness in Christ," so that from this viewpoint we may consider "our disunity as churches." More commonly our disunity is given prior place, at least the concrete situation of separate churches is considered the norm, and if there be interest for the unity of the church it is extracted from the givenness of "divided Christendom." Would it be an exaggeration to say that most Protestants differ very little from the Roman Catholic in holding, consciously or unconsciously, the notion that, if there is to be a unity of the churches, it will only happen when all other Christians "join our church"? Quite different is the attitude of those who believe that in some sense the One Christ is the substratum of all the churches and that the degree in which a church may claim to be a Christian Church depends on its participation in this One Christ. "Our own church" must constantly be judged by its participation in Him, and our relationship to other churches will be seen in His light rather than in the light of historical attractions and repulsions which have resulted in our agreements or our differences. Much of our thinking on the matter of church unity moves in the area of defending relationships which were created in other days, other countries, other contexts, and making these a test of the purity of Christian faith. We do not judge other Christians and other churches directly by their confession of faith but by their relationships to institutions and formulae in some remote time and place. Simple honesty demands that we be willing to hear what our contemporary fellow Christians

[5]

have to say, as well as what was said in the 16th century. There is a temptation to defend the "faith of our fathers" in a way that makes pride in the fathers more decisive than any purity of the faith.

Our disunity as churches is a heritage of history. This is not to say that we would all be one in faith if we had no such heritage. Even if we tried to divest ourselves of our past we could not, but nothing in the history of the church leads us to believe that there ever was a period of complete unity. On the contrary the more we know of the story of the church the less apt we are to believe the romantic Roman theory of a medieval glory when all the faithful were one. The schism between the West and the East goes back to the earliest centuries, and even the first era witnessed a wide variety which was less noticed than in a later period when an attempted uniformity revealed the parts that would not "fit." It is not at all certain that some of the early sects, such as the Montanists, and even the Donatists, were as irregular as the fervent proponents of a unified organization wanted to make them out to be. Early Church history has been written by those who represented the unifying organizers and dissident groups have never been given full justice by the "orthocrats."

But there is nothing sacred about the divisions which have been created in the past. They were the outcome of forces and movements which neither can nor ought to be revived. In a way they were inevitable. It is a naive view of disunity which makes all the present churches "for" or "against" *our* church. One might imagine a great day of decision in the past when all other Christians voted either to accept or reject the Augsburg Confession. But it would be pure imagination. To large numbers of Christians even in 1530 the Augsburg Confession was irrelevant, just as to many other Christians the Westminster Assembly or the Synod of Dort or the Seventh Ecumenical Conference were irrelevant. The actual "breaks" of church territories, as some sort of geological fissure, do not follow any universal simple lines but are the results of a multitude of historical conditions and events where geography, temperament, traditions, leadership, all interplay. For any one unity of Christendom to set itself up as a touchstone of all other Christians is a sort of spiritual pride against which the apostle warned when he urged against thinking of oneself "more highly than he ought to think" (Rom. 12:3—a passage set in a very definite ecumenical context. Cf. v. 5 "we, who are many, are one body in Christ"). Certainly sin has had much to do with all the churches of Christendom, but we ought to distinguish between sinful motives and

[6]

natural purposes. The Church of England is probably as natural an expression as the Dutch Reformed Church, and the Lutheran synods of America belong to the history of the United States as well as the German territorial churches to their provinces. Different church bodies are no more reprehensible than different social structures. Our disunity as churches must be seen in the light of the history of both Eastern and Western Europe. The sin lies not in the variety of organization but in the minds and hearts of people in the organizations. It is conceivable that all Christians might be in one great church—which could engender sins no less sinful than the sins in the smallest sects. The point at which our disunity as churches becomes a betrayal of our faith is where we do not permit our oneness in Christ to express itself in our relationships with other churches.

It would require more study than has been given to the question to discover why Christians have thought themselves more faithful to their Lord in defining their differences than their unity. They have asserted positively that they must be loyal to the trust in their confession of faith, but in elaborating what they believe is true they have stressed usually the points wherein they differ from other Christians, differences they have underscored as "distinctive." It is natural that by such distinctions they have identified themselves, but may they not, in their fervor to make themselves "distinct," have sharpened these differences, or made them important beyond proportion? And have they perchance made the points of difference the vital thing, whereas the points of agreement, if they were equally considered, might prove the more significant for the faith of the church? We need today to re-examine the foundations of our faith, not with the thought of justifying our separatedness—this is the common attitude and approach—but with the thought of justifying our claim to be catholic Christians.

A catholic Christian faith is a whole faith, wherein particular doctrines are related to each other and integrated into a fulness of the New Testament faith. Many of the churches are "pointed" churches, churches which have developed this or that "point" of difference into a system that is clearly "lopsided." We need to reassess the relatedness of all doctrines and decide on which life or death depends—a living or a dead faith—and which admit of varying interpretations. The body of Christ is living, is flexible, not rigid, unyielding, hard. There is even in the fulness of faith a freedom which admits of differences—it is important to define this freedom, this "tolerance."

To take an example which touches on the most sensitive of Lutheran nerves. Lutheran theologians rightly stress the doctrine of the means of grace. Yet they do not hesitate to admit that the unbaptized child may be saved, and that the Eucharist is not absolutely essential. It is possible to be saved even if one has not communicated. Granted that it is not the *use* but the *contempt* of the sacrament which is decisive, does it seem right for Lutherans to brand the Reformed who have other views of the sacraments as "of another spirit," implying another than the Spirit of Christ? Whatever Luther may have meant by the phrase, are we justified in transferring to all others of the Reformed faith today a condemnation that denies fellowship with them? Do we know what our contemporary fellow Christians believe on this matter, or are we applying a sort of legal principle that all the descendants of the 16th century shall be judged by the decisions of that century?

May we not believe that the Spirit of God is working today as in other centuries and is seeking to bring men together around Christ? Shall we deny that this is His purpose and stand in the way of His overcoming the barriers erected in other days? The goal of any church is not the preservation of an ancient arrangement, but a new creation in Christ whereby the old things pass away. This is not to say that we do not possess the truth in our church, but it does mean that the truth is not ours to guard but to use for the redemption of mankind. The distinctions of history become solidified, unworkable, even monumental. We need the Spirit's power to break them up, reshape and revitalize them, praying that out of them may come purer, more universal, more perfect forms than those enshrined in the past. It was in regard to sacrosanct customs that Jesus uttered words that seemed blasphemous to His contemporaries, "My Father worketh even until now, and I work" (John 5:17).

As we think through the theme of our "disunity as churches" and assess all their historical, doctrinal, practical factors—and honesty demands this—we need ever keep in mind "our oneness in Christ"—Christian faith and love demand this. We have become more adept in the former than in the latter. If we face frankly what our oneness in Christ is, we shall have to face the consequence of what this means. We must confess to the world that wherein we are one. We must find ways of expressing that oneness. To say "I believe in one holy catholic and apostolic church" and do nothing about it, is to be guilty of a dead faith, a faith in this instance without works. If we can find little in Church history to help us in giving reality to our oneness in Christ, then we must invent ways and devise structures which will lead men to understand that, though we are separated in various churches, we do belong to a Christ who is not divided. However pure our confessions may be, they are defective and misleading, if they proclaim to the world a Christ who is less than the Christ of the Gospels or different from the Christ who is the one head of the one Church. He is not "our" Christ, we are *His* people, and our proclamation must show Him forth in all His fulness.

Existential examination of denominational differences!

The Realization of Church Fellowship

By Prof. Peter Brunner

THERE ARE MANY signs which indicate that the work of the World Council of Churches has reached a decisive stage. Church bodies are therein joined together through official delegations. The registered tables of agreements and disagreements among these churches may be said now to have been completed. There is also widespread agreement that the churches dare not be satisfied merely with brotherly co-operation in facing practical tasks, valuable as that may be. The sentiment is now expressed: "We must move forward! We dare not lose sight of the goal of the ecumenical movement! This goal is the full union of our divided churches. We must now travel new roads which will bring us closer to this goal!"

Stronger than in earlier years, the ecumenical responsibility is understood today concretely in terms of bringing about a full organic union of divided churches. And already this desire has expressed itself in deed! The Church of South India is an expression of this desire. The events in South India will have repercussions in the home churches involved. Up to now it looked as if the union which took place in South India ultimately involved only the Anglican and some free churches which have emanated from it and were living together with it. But now Lutheran mission churches also seem to be on the verge of entering the fellowship of the Church of South India. In the light of these unity consultations—whatever their final outcome will be—all the home churches of the Lutheran Reformation are called upon to examine whether the way of these mission churches is practicable, and whether perhaps the hour for very far-reaching church union is also near for the European and American home churches.

In this situation a fundamental theological deliberation is necessary. We will only be prepared for the coming practical questions which face us in this new development after we have first reached understanding on their theological implications. We offer the following considerations as a small contribution to this end, and we will conclude with a few practical consequences drawn out of them.

I.

It is one of the happy signs of the renewal in our thinking and teaching on the doctrine of the church that we are aware of a close connection between the New Testament concepts of the "church" and the "kingdom of God." We should try to understand the nature of the church in terms of its connection with the kingdom of God which will come into appearance with the return of Christ on the Day of Judgment. Without an eschatology of the end of history, there is no ecclesiology in keeping with the New Testament message. On this basis, we are led to the following understanding: the church on earth is the community of men which will one day be united in the kingdom of God at the wedding feast of the Lamb on the other side of the resurrection of the dead.

According to Matthew, our Lord spoke the following words at the institution of Holy Communion: "I will not drink henceforth of this fruit of the vine, until that day when I drink it new with you in my Father's kingdom." All those comprise the church who belong to the disciples of Jesus for whom this promise, "with you in my Father's kingdom," is really valid. The church comprises those branches of the vine which are not cut off, thrown away, and burned in the fire, but rather which are purified and bring forth fruit.

The member churches of the World Council of Churches are agreed that in each of the confessional churches, according to God's good pleasure, men may live who will inherit the kingdom of God as living members of the body of Christ. Thereby the World Council of Churches confesses the *una sancta catholica ecclesia.* This church which we confess in our creed is one. It was never divided into multiplicity and can never be so divided. Under "unity of the church," we mean here the numerical unity. In the same way as we confess of God, "one God and not many gods;" and as we confess of Christ, "one Lord and not many lords;" and as we confess of the Holy Ghost, "one Spirit of the one God;" so also we confess of this Church of God that it always was, is, and will be, one. For God's kingdom is one kingdom. Christ is the only true vine. Christ has only one body in which all of His children are members. The unity of the church is unquestionably constantly given. The unity of the spiritual body of Jesus is indestructible. As little as the kingdom of God can fall apart into partial kingdoms because of the oneness of God, so little can the body of Christ be torn apart, for the head of the body is one.

When we take this seriously, we cannot formulate our task in the ecumenical consultations to be the establishing of the unity of the Church of Jesus Christ. Contrariwise, we must derive our ecumenical obligation from the unity of the church that is continually given. We should not formulate our task in such a way as to say that we have to make the unity of the church of God visible on earth. For we cannot visibly draw the lines of division which truly separate the living members of the body of Jesus from those who will not inherit the kingdom of God. This line of separation is seen now only by the eye of God. Therefore the unity of the Church of God will only first be manifest for our eyes in the apocalyptic revelation of the kingdom of God.

Before we can properly describe the ecumenical task which grows out of the already existing and continually realized unity of the church, we must first pause a moment to consider the essential marks of the church which we confess in our creed.

We believe the one church to be holy. If the one church is the community of those who will inherit the kingdom of God as the living members of the body of Jesus, then the church, by necessity of its very nature, is already holy. Holiness means here: to belong to God and His kingdom, to be called out of the world, to be freed of the tyrannical bondage of evil powers, to belong to the Lord Jesus Christ as His body, to be truly in Christ, to be wholly covered with the righteousness of Christ, to partake of the life of God. The holiness of the church is incorporated into the unity which it enjoys in the one head and in the one kingdom of the Father.

We have already seen that the unity of the church is indestructible. Therefore the totality of this church as an indestructible spiritual reality is also guaranteed. The head does not allow any of the living members of its body to be severed. Neither sex, nor race, neither nationality, nor office, nor caste, nor levitical ritual, nor canon

[13]

law, nor political or geographical boundaries, nor any earthly condition at all— even physical death—may attack or dissolve the unity and holiness of the church which is in Christ. The Church of God—without detriment to its growth—is totally indestructible in each Now. Therefore we confess this one holy church as catholic. The indestructible spiritual totality of the church is the nature of its catholicity. When we confess the church as all-encompassing, as catholic, then we mean to confess just this indestructible integrity of the church which is necessarily given with its unity and holiness.

The unity, holiness, and catholicity of the church are very closely related to each other. One follows out of the other, because they are already incorporated within each other. At bottom, all three of these true marks of the church are one. They all characterize the one spiritual body of Jesus Christ.

For our theological thinking, the doctrine of the church would be much easier to master, if we could limit its marks to unity, holiness, and catholicity. In our ecumenical conversations, the tasks, goals, and means would be much easier to determine, if we were able to confine ourselves to the reality of the church as one, holy, and catholic. But our creed goes further and confesses the one, holy, catholic church as apostolic. (Herein lie the peculiar knots in theological ecclesiology as well as the deepest *aporia* in ecumenical practice.

One may be permitted to ask the question whether our ecumenical conversations have seriously considered the fact that the one, holy, catholic church as such is also apostolic? The difficulty and distress which the mark of apostolicity causes us—but also the promise which is inherent therein—consist in the fact that the apostolicity of the *una sancta catholica ecclesia* places it squarely within the history of the world. The unity, holiness, and catholicity of the church partake of the invisibility of the eschatological boundary lines which divide the redeemed members of the body of Jesus from those branches cut off and thrown away. But the mark of apostolicity must have something to do with the apostles of Jesus Christ. These apostles are historical. The apostolic, therefore, must be something like the unity, holiness, and catholicity which comes certainly from the Lord, but must also be something which comes from the historical Jesus through the historical apostles, and thereby also through the history of the church on earth. If our ecclesiology is to be true to the witness of the New Testament, then it must unite these two lines within itself: (1) a spiritual-charismatic line which includes everything which is to be said of the church as the body of the Exalted One as breathed through by

[14]

the Holy Ghost, and (2) an historical line within the world which includes all that is characterized as apostolic. We have once again become certain of the spiritual-charismatic content of ecclesiology in our ecumenical discussions. But are we as clear as to what we mean when we confess with the same breath the *una sancta catholica* and *apostolica ecclesia?*

The concept of apostolicity is itself a complex one in connection with the concept of the church. The relation of the apostolicity of the church to its unity, holiness, and catholicity is likewise many-sided. We must limit ourselves here to what is decisive. The constitutive element in the mark of apostolicity lies in its certified fidelity to the witness of the apostles.

The church is apostolic in so far as it is sent out to the peoples of the world with the witness of Christ which has come directly from the mouths of the apostles. Sending and Word: both together in an inseparable unity provide the church with its apostolicity. The apostolicity of the sending rests finally upon the apostolicity of the Word which is proclaimed via the sending. We must ask ourselves what our fidelity to the apostolicity of the Word means for the ecclesiological significance of the sending. The questions dare not be disregarded here which are asked of us by the episcopally-constituted churches within the World Council of Churches. But any *nuda successio* of the office which disregards the critical norm of the apostolic in view of the content of the Word proclaimed by the messengers is a caricature of apostolicity. Would it not be a regression to the kind of Judaism battled by Paul, if one wanted to make the mark of apostolicity depend solely upon the existence of a *successio* of the office as mediated by the laying on of hands? The demand to preserve the apostolic Word necessitates, in times of emergency, a break with the demand to maintain community with an historical episcopate. This is the painful—but liberating—lesson which the Lutheran Reformation had to learn. The church is apostolic when it is truly evangelical. And the church is truly evangelical when the content of its message is substantially identical with the message which was proclaimed by the commissioned eyewitnesses of the Easter appearance of Jesus. The church is apostolic when it allows its proclamation to be judged by the witness which is composed and comprehended in the prophetic and apostolic writings of the Old and New Testaments.

To measure properly the importance of this apostolicity of the church, we must ask what its relation is to the other marks of the church. Certainly the sentence is valid that the one, holy, catholic church is sent to the peoples of the world with the Word of the apostles and the prophets. Certainly the sentence is also valid that the office of preaching reconciliation is instituted in the one, holy, catholic church. On the other hand, however, it must be noted that the apostles belong to the foundation of the church. The call to witness to the Resurrected One occurs through an historical act of Jesus appearing at Easter. This is before the church, born of Word and sacrament, is erected out of Jews and Gentiles into the unity of the body of Christ. Through the Word of the called witnesses, the one people of God is gathered from Jews and Gentiles. Through the *ministerium verbi*, as through an instrument, God gives the implanted Spirit and faith to the body of Christ. The one, holy, catholic church is no invisible *civitas platonica*, but lives as an historical reality in the circle of the apostolic gospel and the sacraments transmitted by the apostles. Jesus Christ builds the one, holy, catholic church as his spiritual body in the power of the Father, via the Holy Ghost, and through the visible, historical realities of the proclamation of the Word and the administration of the sacraments. Therefore the mark of apostolicity—in the realm of the historically comprehensible—provides the concrete place where I may believe the presence of the one, holy, catholic church to be. To this extent, the apostolicity is fundamentally necessary for the being and knowledge of the unity, holiness, and catholicity of the church. Only through the *ministerium verbi* is a man reborn as a living member of the body of Christ, and because of this, the place is bounded where, through the efficacy of the *ministerium verbi*, I may be certain of the presence of the spiritual body of Jesus.

II.

With these last sentences we stand before the historical fact of divided churches. Christians are not agreed in their answer to the question concerning the significance of the apostolicity of the church. Even those Christians who are agreed that apostolicity consists essentially in the preservation of the apostolic Word and sacraments are not agreed as to what the normative content of the apostolic Word and sacraments really is. The place where Christians of this world acknowledge the mark of apostolicity at its clearest and purest is not the same for all. Therefore the churches are divided. There may be other grounds for church division, but those divisions which are theologically meaningful (and thereby most difficult) are those which issue from disagreement on the mark of apostolicity. In the contemporary situation of Christianity, each of us is faced with the decision as to whether to issue a No to other churches within the World Council of Churches in regard to their understanding of the church's apostolicity. (The decision for apostolicity has necessarily become a decision for a confessional church.) Even those who hold the widest possible union to be desirable, must make their acceptance of apostolicity dependent upon their decision for a confession as long as they recognize other true members of the body of Jesus which belong to a church structure (as, for example, the Roman Catholic) which they themselves cannot join.

Dare we be satisfied with this situation? Certainly we may comfort ourselves with the indestructible spiritual unity of the body of Jesus. Certainly our disunity regarding the apostolic cannot abrogate our unity in Christ as long as we are really living members of His body. Certainly we may comfort ourselves with the fact that basic apostolic elements have been preserved in the churches gathered together in the ecumenical movement—and in the Church of Rome itself—such as baptism, the instruction of the Ten Commandments, the Apostles' Creed, the Lord's Prayer, the Holy Scriptures of the Bible, and their reading in divine service. We are thereby convinced that also in the churches divided from us we find apostolic elements, and men who live in the body of Christ, by God's grace, who will one day inherit the kingdom of God. And certainly we may be thankful for the intensive community of work among the member churches of the World Council of Churches, bound together in loving social service in the alleviation of manifold emergencies. Thereby we experience something of the spiritual and corporal brotherhood in Christ. But we dare not console ourselves too greatly.

We would misinterpret the unity of the church which we have described if we had a good conscience about the existing divisions among the churches. Precisely because the unity of the church is spiritual, it intervenes in the empirical situation of the divided churches. That which is valid for the Holy Spirit drives to realize itself in concrete existence. The Spirit yearns for corporeality. Therefore, the given spiritual unity of the *sancta catholica ecclesia* works with the necessity of a *dynamis* of the Holy Spirit on the form and corporate life of the local *ecclesiae*.

But how should this spiritual unity be reflected in the historical forms of the hearing and proclaiming church? How do we really formulate the goal which we wish to reach with our ecumenical efforts?

It is easy to formulate negatively: the overcoming of the divisions which now exist among the divided confessions. What does this mean

[17]

positively? Certainly this—the divided churches should unite. United churches or perhaps even a single united church should be realized on earth. But what do we mean by united churches or a single united church? Something like a unified church with a central world church leadership, perhaps not so completely centralized as the Roman Catholic church, but still a church which has its central, all-inclusive church government at one place on earth? Or do we think of the full general assembly of the World Council of Churches meeting here and there, solidifying itself into a world synod which, through its resolutions, would lead all its member churches right out to the farthest reaches of Africa and Asia? Or are we of the opinion that through mutual sacramental fellowship, the spiritual unity of the body of Christ in history is already adequately effected, needing no more beyond this than the loose fellowship in the World Council of Churches? Or, with the Anglican theologians, do we aim for a visible band of unity among all churches of the world by a common incorporation into the historic episcopate and its peculiar ordination, so that perhaps a world council of bishops standing in the apostolic succession would be the symbolical expression of the united church of God on earth?

We will have to avoid two extreme answers to this question. On the one hand, we dare not seek the overcoming of the divisions among our churches in a united legal system of government which brings together all the congregations and churches under a single leading summit, however it might be formed. This is the one extreme. On the other hand, we dare not console ourselves merely with an arrangement of mutual admission to Holy Communion and see in it alone the overcoming of the divisions. That would be the second extreme. The status in which the spiritual unity of the church is reflected in history is richer, more manifold and far-reaching, than simply mutual admission to Holy Communion. Above all, we have to beware of lifting out something singular and declaring that agreement there would document union. Rather, we must realize that church union manifests itself through an abundance of actually lived, concrete, historical, and of course, legally formulated relationships and forms of expression. I suggest the word "church fellowship" *(Kirchengemeinschaft)* as incorporating all of these elements.

The continually realized and indestructible unity of the church in the spiritual body of Christ corresponds to the *koinonia* of the churches of God on earth.

There is also a completely legitimate plurality of churches. But all local *ecclesiae* in the whole world should stand in a concrete, actually lived, legally effective *koinonia.* Such a local church can also be an *autocephalous* established church and still stand, undetrimental to its ecclesiastical self-control, in *koinonia* with other *autocephalous* churches.

If we inquire concerning the forms of expression of this church fellowship, then we will certainly begin with mutual admission to Holy Communion as a fundamental form of *koinonia.* But we dare not remain at this level. To church fellowship also belongs necessarily a full pulpit and altar fellowship. Implicit in this is a mutual recognition of ordinations among churches. The nature of church fellowship also demands that it be expressed formally. One must know between which churches it obtains, for conditions may arise which would demand its abrogation.

We should not predetermine the boundaries of the multiplicity of forms and fruits of the Spirit in which this *koinonia* among the churches expresses itself. For example, why cannot a freely consummated inclusion into the fellowship of the historical episcopate also be a fitting form of expression in such church fellowship? The significance of the offering of the Pauline congregations for the preservation of church fellowship with the mother church in Jerusalem should be remembered in this connection. Was not the apostle himself, through his person and office, a decisive element in the early Christian *koinonia* among the churches? What would be its current expression?

The basic element which is the *conditio sine qua non* for the realization of church fellowship, however, we have not yet named. It is the matter of apostolicity upon which the realization of church fellowship depends. Churches which live among each other in *koinonia* must mutually acknowledge the mark of apostolicity in them. Only apostolic *ecclesiae* can live in church fellowship with each other. In the light of our definition of apostolicity, we must make this sentence so concrete as to say: Only those churches which agree in their hearing and proclaiming of the apostolic Word as to what they hear and proclaim can be in *koinonia* with each other. Church fellowship, therefore, includes a common acknowledgement of the doctrinal decisions made concerning the content of the apostolic gospel. Church fellowship is confessional fellowship.

Why must we confess this agreement in the hearing and proclaiming of the gospel as the foundation of all church fellowship? Why cannot we be satisfied with a certain minimum, say a broadening of the theological basis of the World Council of Churches to which many churches could certainly agree? Why cannot we share church fellowship with churches in which we recognize certain valid elements of apostolicity, but which are mixed with other anti-apostolic teachings? To these questions there can be only one decisive, conscience-binding theological answer—because the apostolicity of the church is the working foundation for the unity holiness, and catholicity of the church.

This answer may be further developed. The apostolic gospel and the administration of the sacraments as expressing that gospel are the means entrusted to Christians through which God saves men from eternal lostness and through which He sends the Spirit and faith. Therefore these means dare not be impugned. Where they are impugned, it becomes difficult for men to come to a saving faith. Where they are totally destroyed, it becomes impossible for men to come to a saving faith. For the sake of men's salvation, the church stands under the command to preserve clearly the apostolic Word, and thereby, the mark of apostolicity at its center. In obedience to this principal ecclesiological command, the church must repudiate all false doctrine. In obedience to this command, it must refuse to grant church fellowship where agreement cannot be reached on the content of the Word which is to be proclaimed as the apostolic message and faithfully administered in its sacraments.

Thereby we stand in the midst of the serious crisis in which our churches find themselves because of our lack of illumination and the situation obtaining in our theological sciences. Is it still possible to draw a clear boundary line between apostolic and heretical? Cannot all confessions somehow point back to the New Testament for their peculiar doctrinal teachings? Do not all members of the World Council of Churches put up with convictions among their pastors, professors, and church leaders which the fathers of these churches have repudiated as heretical? This distressing situation is known to us all, and we must understand it properly. It would be to misunderstand our situation today, were we to make a kind of virtue out of it, saying, "Since we can no longer determine the boundary line between apostolic and heretical, we must push the question concerning agreement on the hearing and proclaiming of the content of the apostolic message into the background, and take instead the preponderant organizational road to solve the problem of church fellowship. The lines of division which our fathers saw have become largely historical ballast, especially for the mission churches. The progress of the history of ideas and theology has freed us from this ballast. What hinders us from viewing this question of agreement on the apostolic Word completely anew? What would hinder us from bypassing all questions of substantial doctrinal content—except for a somewhat broadened theological "basis" of the World Council of Churches—and perhaps seek instead an agreement on practical deeds through which the apostolicity of the involved churches could be demonstrated?"

Those who think in this fashion have misunderstood the need of our churches today. Whoever thinks this way has taken a decisive step toward the dissolution of the church. The extent to which the living apostolic Word becomes silent in separating the truth of God from the error of man is the extent to which the true nature of the church is placed in question. If, in our present cultural and theological situation, it is difficult to hear the apostolic Word in its binding unity, purity, and clarity (and thereby to hear its power to unmask heresy), then it is a sign that God is punishing us. If we have no power to distinguish the apostolic from the anti-apostolic Word, then there hovers over us a cloud of godly wrath. All attempts to realize church fellowship by skirting the question of agreement on the apostolic gospel stand from the very outset under the judgment of God.

What should we do in this situation? First, we should honestly face and acknowledge the gravity of the crisis in which we find ourselves. Were we to do this, we would ask God above all for His Holy Spirit, so that He would reveal the Word of His apostolic witnesses to the congregations gathered for worship, and distinguish the apostolic from the heretical. Furthermore — burdened with this need — we should still risk coming together with our neighboring churches for serious discussions on how we hear the apostolic witness. We must take this risk. If the mark of apostolicity really is fundamental for the proclamation of church fellowship, then at no point in the ecumenical movement should we want to effect church fellowship in the sense described above, without first reaching a public consensus as to how, here and now, we hear the apostolic Word in just this critical area. Churches which are divided because of dissension over the understanding of the apostolic Word can only overcome this division by finding again the lost consensus on doctrinal agreement. Conversations between churches which are doctrinally divided with the goal of reaching doctrinal agreement is the one absolutely decisive means of fulfilling our ecumenical obligations.

I shall bring our convictions here to a close. I am sure that especially for a confessionally-bound church, new and important questions break through at this point. I am convinced, however, that even these questions can be fundamentally solved by a consideration of the relation between the confession now prevailing and future doctrinal agreements. But this task stands elsewhere. Before we venture to undertake it, unanimity should prevail on the following theses which condense the points I have made which I consider to be of fundamental importance.

(1)   The already existing spiritual unity of the Church of Jesus Christ demands the realization of concrete, historical, tangible church fellowship.

(2)   Church fellowship realizes itself in a variety of forms of expression. Full pulpit and altar fellowship and unlimited recognition of ordinations are constitutive elements of such church fellowship.

(3)   Only apostolic churches can realize church fellowship with each other.

(4)   Those churches are apostolic which preserve the gospel orally testified by the Apostles by their public doctrine, guard themselves against contamination with heresy, and which see to it that this teaching is locally proclaimed.

(5)   Any attempt to realize church fellowship without facing the question of the apostolicity of the churches involved is doomed to failure.

(6)   The only promising way—despite weakness and distress—is to assume responsibility for binding doctrinal conversations among the churches, aiming toward the goal of doctrinal agreement on what we today hear, proclaim, and openly confess to be the binding content of the apostolic Word.

(7)   Those churches in the World Council of Churches which consider themselves to be confessionally kindred churches are called upon today to enter into such binding conversations with each other for the sake of Christ.

Doctrinal Formulations

BY PROF. MARTIN J. HEINECKEN

As I CONCEIVE THE PROBLEM before us it is this: What is the relation between the inner unity of those who have been taken hold of by Christ, and who feel that they are one with all who have been similarly apprehended, and the doctrinal formulations in which this inner unity of faith must now also come to expression?

Or in other words: When men meet on life's way and, in the struggle with other lords that also make their claim upon them, discover their common allegiance to the same Lord and become convinced that they are at one in their basic orientation, then how much agreement must there be in the way in which this feeling of oneness also comes to theological expression before you can say that the inner unity really exists?

It is the problem facing the ecumenical church in its conversations across the lines of the denominations. It is the problem posed by the seventh article of the Augsburg Confession (*ad veram unitatem ecclesiae satis est consentire de doctrina evangelii et administratione sacramentorum. Nec necesse est ubique esse similes traditiones humanas seu ritus aut ceremonias ab hominibus institutas*). What is this *satis est* upon which it is necessary to insist, if that which is vital is not to be forfeited, and beyond which one is not to go if one is not to become guilty of narrow orthodoxy? Where is the dividing line between what is essential to the gospel and what are merely human traditions, rites, and ceremonies? Are there or are there not "adiaphora" and if there are, what are they? This is the problem with which we must wrestle if we are really to present a united front to a common foe, and are not to be misled by sentimentality into easy but specious agreement or by pride into narrow exclusiveness.

As I see it on the American scene, at the grass roots where this thing must come to fruition, midst a variety of variations, it is easy to establish two extremes:

1. At the one extreme, men are still quite satisfied with a mere feeling of unity. They seem to have learned nothing from the course which human events have taken of late. It can be expressed quite popularly: "It doesn't make any difference what you believe, just so you believe." Sincerity alone matters ("We are all headed for the same place anyway, and there are many roads that lead to the same goal."). This is the *fides qua creditur* to the exclusion of the *fides quae*. It is a radical misunderstanding of Kirkegaard's challenging assertion that "subjectivity is truth." A certain "religious experience" in distinction from other experiences, aesthetic and the like, is the only important thing and if you feel that you share this experience, much in the same way that two people share a common appreciation of the beauties of nature, without however expressing themselves in the same way about it, that is all that is necessary. It is sort of a matter of taste. You notice that you have similar tastes, and you rejoice and let it go at that.

Or perhaps someone says: "It really doesn't make any difference what you believe, but everything depends on how you live; and if only people will treat each other decently and humanely, and act in accordance with the universally acceptable 'golden rule,' they can believe what they like about all those nebulous and speculative matters to which it is impossible to find definite answers in any case." It is the practical, pragmatic attitude. Whatever works is true. The important thing is unity in action.

2. Quite at the other extreme, then, we find those who recognize no sort of unity in faith unless there is complete agreement in every detail of an entire system of dogmatics. So there are no "adiaphora," and no so-called "open questions," concerning which two people may differ amicably, although of the same household of faith. Before you can have pulpit and altar fellowship, therefore, even before you can pray together, there must be agreement in all details, inclusive, e.g.,

[24]

of the *communicatio idiomatum* with its three genera, *idiomaticum, majestaticum, apotelesmaticum.* I might refer, e.g., to F. Pieper's Dogmatics (Vol. II), where the discussion of the *communicatio idiomatum* extends over 150 pages, while the resurrection of Jesus is not even indicated in the table of contents, and is then polished off in exactly two pages and eight lines. This is done, moreover, entirely in Aristotelian categories, mentioning the *causa efficiens,* and the resurrection *clauso sepulchro* to correspond with the birth *clauso utero* (thereby to refute the Reformed heresy which restricts the presence of the body of Christ to the *praesentia visibilis et localis.* Incidentally, I do not mean to infer that there are not real issues here with which we must certainly come to terms. I only mean to cite examples of an extreme view. So one insists that the pope is the antichrist, one denies the *praedestinatio intuitu fidei,* and makes them essential to unity.)

Somewhere between these two extremes the truth must lie, but it must be achieved, it seems to me, not by any sort of compromise but by a different orientation. It must be shown, it would seem to me, that it is not a quantitative, but a qualitative matter. It is a matter of how the gospel is basically understood. As Bishop Nygren says, it is a matter of the dominant motif and of the whole orientation on that basis, in other words, of how the God relationship is conceived. It is a matter of the fundamental answer to the fundamental question as to how the God relationship is established and maintained, and then of allowing this basic answer really to dominate and to penetrate into every nook and cranny of what is believed and said.

I think we may learn from what Kierkegaard says concerning the stages of life. This is not a quantitative but a qualitative matter, so that one cannot pass from one stage to the other by gradual degrees but only by a qualitative, all-at-once leap. No matter what one's profession may be, and no matter whether one does on occasion seem to do the good for its own sake, it soon becomes apparent in the pinches, whether or not a man really lives in aesthetic or ethical categories; whether he really lives only for the moment, or has already leaped over into a new quality of life where he now lives, not for the moment, but for the eternal, i.e., in accord with immutable, universal principle. And then again, it is a matter of passing by the same kind of qualitative leap from the stage of immanent religiosity, where the truth is found within, to that of the specifically Christian. Do you find God within the depths of your being in a fundamental integrity (*ubique et nusquam*), or must God come to you from the outside at a time and place through Word and sacrament? Can you give birth to the truth that is within you with the aid only of a Socratic midwife, or must the truth be begotten in you by that one whose sole prerogative it is to beget the truth? If this re-creation and rebirth have taken place, then the whole quality of life becomes different, and this new quality will permeate every aspect of it. So that it is not at all a matter of discerning quantitatively whether there is agreement on, let us say, 60 percent or 90 percent, but whether or not there is really the new quality of understanding and of actual living.

The same can be illustrated from the *eros, nomos, agape* motif distinctions. There could be a high degree of quantitative agreement in many isolated doctrines between two people, and yet they may disagree basically in their understanding of the gospel and may be living at qualitatively different levels, because they give a basically different answer to the fundamental question as to how the God relation is established and maintained. It is by ferreting out this basic orientation that it will be established whether or not there is any real unity in faith.

So, the difference between the Lutheran or Evangelical position and the Roman Catholics is a matter of total orientation, all of one piece, and you cannot say that there is agreement on some doctrines, and disagreement on others. This is where I believe the Augsburg Confession may help to create confusion when it gives the impression, at least, that there is agreement on some points and not on others. Because they disagreed at the heart upon the way in which the God relationship is established, they disagreed also on the doctrine of the Trinity and of the person of Christ, even though they accepted the same formulas. Because Luther had really broken with the Aristotelian system of Aquinas, this reached into every nook and cranny. It made no difference now which specific doctrine or which specific ethical problem might come into consideration; it would be different because the total orientation was different. To use only one illustration: If grace is a power infused and you become good by doing good with the help of the infused powers of which the hierarchical church has the monopoly, this is one total orientation, inclusive of dogmatics, ethics, and apologetics, which are all one. If grace is God in His loving disposition to man, accepting the sinner unconditionally; and if you must first become good before you can do good; and if this happens only in the encounter with the living Christ, then you have an altogether different orientation.

It seems to me that it is also the same with Luther and Zwingli, and the later differences between Lutherans and Calvinists. If Luther indicated at Marburg that Zwingli had a different spirit from his, to my mind at least, it does not mean simply that he had a different temperament, as men differ from each other because of a difference in the inherited emotional tone, or because their glands function differently. If this had been all, they might have lived amicably together, and each enriched the other by their different temperaments. But, as a matter of fact, they had a basically different view of the gospel and of how God relates himself to men, and this only came to clear focus in the discussions concerning the Lord's Supper. The vital difference was, therefore, not concerning a peripheral doctrine, but it concerned the very heart and soul of the gospel itself.

The same, it seems to me, is true of Lutherans and Calvinists. It does not seem fairly to represent the issue, if it is said that for Calvin God's sovereignty was primary, while for Luther it was God's love. Luther, too, insisted upon the absolute sovereignty of God, while Calvin also insisted upon the unconditional love of God, as is apparent in his doctrine of absolute predestination. Yet there is a basic difference at this point, and the legalistic spirit of subsequent Calvinism is the proof of it. For Luther it was always God's love that was absolutely sovereign, and this is reflected in his conception of Christian liberty and his repudiation of the third use of the law.

The same basic difference also applies to the *finitum est capax infiniti*. Taken quite seriously, this makes a tremendous difference, and the dispute over the "Real" Presence in the Sacrament, and over the *communicatio idiomatum*, ceases then to be a theological quibble but reaches to the very heart and center of the God-man relationship, and of how the Christian life is to be lived in this world. It involves the whole attitude toward creation, toward the material "thing," toward the treasures of the earth. It might even have something very decisive to say about how we solve the problem of the splitting of the atom.

So I should like to sum up what I have said in the following basic thesis:

Unity of faith does not depend upon the quantitative degree of agreement upon an aggregate of separate doctrines, but it is a qualitative matter of the total orientation and total understanding of the gospel and of the way in which the God relationship is established and maintained. This will make nothing a matter of indifference in so far as it is really related to the center, and is part of the total orientation.

Now I do not intend to develop a whole system of dogmatics, but it does seem to me necessary to lead up to this main thesis with a few other affirmations. Perhaps these are accepted as a matter of course, but at least I want to make my own position clear.

1.   The existential faith relationship to the living Christ is always primary. Being a Christian does not mean the mere acceptance of certain doctrines, but it means being transformed in existence in the encounter with the living Christ. All who have been thus transformed are a part of the "hidden church," the body of Christ. They are contemporary with the living Christ in faith and thus are in the right God and man relationship of trust and love.

Perhaps this will only betray how much I have been influenced by Kierkegaard, but since Kierkegaard wanted no followers, but only meant to expound what it really means to be a Christian, it is for that reason alone that I have adopted his terminology. The *notitia, assensus, fiducia* orientation does not fit. You do not first know with the top of the head, and then assent, and then get around to trusting; but the entire man in his existence is claimed in such a way that he must either surrender in faith or revolt in disobedience. There is no calm spectator assent or dissent. When even the devils believe they tremble. Christianity, therefore, is an existential transformation, of the entire man, in his situation in the dread and insecurity and guilt and tragedy of his existence. It is not a "Weltanschauung" or an intellectually satisfying philosophy of life. It is something quite different; it is incorporation into the body of Christ.

2.   This transformation of existence, however, is not possible without the word of personal address which calls to decision. This word is addressed to the entire person in his existence and must be understood so that a person may respond (either in faith or offense) to the absolute claim made upon him. Hence "the Word was made flesh and dwelt among us."

This is only to stress what it means to be a center of responsibility, a person, created in the image of God. It stresses the I-Thou rather than the I-It relation, to use the modern jargon. The only way in which persons can communicate is through the word. This word must be understood, it must present man with a choice, and call him to decision. The existential transformation is not, therefore, a matter of entering into some kind of atmosphere which subtly changes you without your being aware of it, as when you fall under the spell of beauty or are subtly drawn by some siren song. It was not enough, therefore, that God should be immediately present in the masks of creation. No, God must become incarnate, and must speak to man. He must act. Yes, but actions alone are dumb. So he must also speak.

But this speaking must again be converted into action, for words that are merely on the lips are nothing but sound and fury. So there was no other way, "The Word was made flesh, and dwelt among us (and we beheld his glory, the glory of the only begotten of the Father), full of grace and truth."

3. Thus, while the formulations and acceptance of doctrines are not to be equated with the personal faith relationship, they are inseparable from the formulation of certain doctrines. Not any proclamation or confession will suffice. What is said (in proclamation and confession) must really proclaim the saving gospel; it must say the right thing.

It seems to me that American Protestantism is at last losing its fear of dogma. When it is confronted by Communist dogma that challenges its own cherished way of life, then it suddenly awakens to a consciousness of the importance of doctrine. It is really quite nonsensical to try to separate the *personal* faith relationship from the clear and unequivocal statement of what it is that is believed. The *fides qua creditur* is inseparable from the *fides quae creditur*. Everyone lives in accordance with what he believes and he must be able to put that which he believes into words, even if he uses words to make clear that he does not understand. The mystery of the faith is no mystery, unless it is made clear by the use of words that it is a mystery. Moreover, the gospel is news, and whoever heard of news that was not precisely reported? Everything depends upon the accuracy of the report. So the personal faith relationship is quite inseparable from certain doctrines. There never was a man madly in love who did not sing the praises of his beloved.

4. Such doctrinal formulations are always addressed to a situation, and are meaningful only in that context. They mean to refute certain alternative views, and are thus always apologetic statements.

As every dogmatic assertion is also an ethical one, so it is at the same time an apologetic one. The message and the situation are inseparable. If Jesus is Savior, it must be clear from *what* He saves. If He is Messiah, come to set His people free, it must be clear what the nature of the bondage is, and the Roman taskmaster must not be confused with a different taskmaster. If Jesus is Lord, then other lords must be repudiated, and it must be clear what they are. Doctrinal formulations always arise in a fighting situation, and they must be understood in that context.

5. At the same time all doctrinal formulations are ethical assertions, since belief and actions are inseparable. What the Christian be-

lieves finds expression in his actions. Thus dogmatics, ethics, and apologetics are one, and are treated separately only for practical reasons. This we have already stated and it is repeated here only for the sake of the record.

6. It follows then that the New Testament is the written precipitate of the first witness, and is as such normative for all subsequent proclamation and doctrinal formulations. It is addressed to a situation, and is apologetic in character, and must always be understood in its context. This is to state unequivocally the authoritativeness of the written Scriptures. We are dependent upon them; they are our final court of appeal. We cannot get behind them to reconstruct something that might suit us better. We must accept them for what they are. The New Testament is mentioned in this context, because it is decisive. But this does not mean to deprecate or to exclude the Old Testament; the New Testament must be understood in the light of the Old, just as the Old stands revealed only in the light of the New. There is this inevitable dialectic. This emphasizes again that the New Testament must be understood in its context. This means the whole context of the world into which it came, and this, of course, includes the Old Testament as well as the pagan world surrounding it. The New Testament, then, both corrects and fulfills what is found there.

7. So: The New Testament is not biography or speculative philosophy, but testimony to certain historical events which, however, have a special significance for those who have been transformed in faith. The events to which the writers witness are unique and incomparable, and have a unique significance apprehended only by those themselves transformed in their existence. This, I believe, needs no further comment. The resurrection, e.g., is an historical event, but its significance as a cosmic victory is witnessed to and apprehended only in faith.

8. Hence Kierkegaard, I believe, is right: All the affirmations of faith—whether the witnesses themselves realize this or not—are paradoxical. They are so stated that they can never be merely accepted or else doubted with the intellect on the strength of the evidence, but each puts its claim upon man's existence and sets him before the decision of either "faith" or "offense." They are neither truths of the reason accepted on a priori grounds, nor are they simply historical events, accepted on the basis of good evidence; but they require the transformation of existence whereby the right God relationship is established.

This takes us back again to where we started: the existential faith relationship. If the Christian doctrines, creation, sin, faith, etc., are all paradoxical, it follows that they cannot be accepted in spectator fashion. The paradox is the category which expresses the relation between an existing individual and the nonexisting God, and it forces all man's energies into submission and trust, and keeps him from a mere intellectual acceptance. This understanding is quite basic to the view here presented.

9. If the gospel is thus always addressed to a situation, some questions arise, and the following must be asserted: The human situation into which Christ came, and to which the gospel continues to address itself, is in one sense perennially the same; and those transformed by the living Christ are able, in the light of that encounter and transformation, to diagnose correctly the predicament which the gospel alone meets. This is not the time to give the analysis of the human situation which is always the same. It does not involve an acceptance of all of existential philosophy. It really has nothing to do with present-day so-called existentialism. It means only seeing existence from the vantage point of having been apprehended in Christ. Then it is known what it means to exist before the living God. It is sufficient, then, simply to stress that the human situation to which the gospel addresses itself is at all times and places the same. Existence does not change its essential character.

Nevertheless, it must also be said:

10. Though the essential human situation remains the same, the actual situation of man varies at different times and places and with different cultures. Ways of thinking vary and the whole manner of living will accentuate different problems at different times. To each situation the gospel must be made relevant and all the implications of the gospel worked out in opposition to the prevailing alternatives.

It seems to me that this, too, is clear. The twentieth century is not the sixteenth or the first. The discovery of the compass and the telescope, the discovery of new worlds to conquer, the end of persecution and the beginning of the state church, the rise of nationalism, the beginning of the machine age, Communism, the splitting of the atom, and a thousand and one other things, always create a new situation which the church must meet. How can there be any argument about this? To each situation the gospel must be made relevant and a formulation that met one challenge may not meet the new situation any more than you can stop an atom bomb with a leather shield. Nevertheless, it is the unchanging gospel that must be proclaimed.

11.   Now it must also be pointed out that what the gospel offers does not mean only a quantitative change. Hence the thesis: The transition from Judaism to Christianity (from Old Testament to New Testament), or from paganism (the natural man) to Christianity is never a matter of mere quantitative increment but of qualitative correction and transformation. It is not a matter of adding certain new doctrines to those already held, and of adding certain principles of conduct to those already accepted, but both doctrines and actions become transformed in a new context.

Now, we are again returning to the main thesis. There must be a break with the first and second story view of natural and revealed theology held by Roman Catholics. There must be the qualitative break from old to new. You do not just add more stuff when you pass from cotton to silk. Silk has a different origin and, therefore, a different quality. So also it is with the religion of the old man and the transformation of the one who is apprehended by Christic. There is fulfillment here, but there is always first the radical correction. This, too, is basic.

12.   Hence, in the light of all the foregoing, there can be no fixation of theology in a system adequate for all times and places. This is the mistake of Thomism with its system of Aristotelian categories, with which the Reformation broke and to which the seventeenth century orthodoxy returned, thus destroying the existential character of the affirmations of faith. Perhaps I am overly sensitive at this point, but having been brought up to know nothing but the seventeenth century orthodoxy until very recently, I may perhaps be excused a little ranting. If there is one system of theology adequate for all times, then we cannot do better than to accept Thomism. Here is the Latin language, dead as a dodo, unchanging, fixed for all time, here is the philosophy of Aristotle, providing the frame of reference. Once having accepted it, we can add to it quantitatively, and end up worshiping Mary as the Mother of God. All this makes wonderful sense, once you grant the premises. But if we are going to break with Aristotle, we must do a good job and not stop halfway. Fortunately the adherents of the seventeenth century orthodoxy were in their lives as Christians much better than their theology. Today perhaps it is the reverse. Nevertheless, the issue of the Reformation is quite clear, and we face the either-or, either one fixated system of theology adequate for all times and needing only periodic supplementation, or else a constant restatement of the one unchanging gospel.

But then it must be clear what is meant by a "system of theology."

13. By a "system of theology" is not to be understood a rational system deduced from a priori principles on which there would be universal agreement on the basis of man's rationality. We are all aware of the attempt of Descartes and others to find in answer to the existential dread of life the same kind of apodictic certainty that he found in mathematics in answer to a speculative doubt. In answer to this attempt it is enough, it seems to me, simply to say with Kierkegaard that life is not a system, and that you can get apodictic certainty only when you abstract completely from existence. For life, such a rational system is then, of course, excluded.

14. Neither is it a system in the sense that it brings together the sum total of man's experience into a coherent system tested by the law of contradiction and the weight of the evidence. Here, too, Kierkegaard's answer can be given: Life is not a system, and, above all, Christianity is not a "Weltanschauung." We must leave such speculations for those who have the leisure for them. He who is under orders to proclaim the gospel will have no time for them.

15. Finally, it is also not a system in the sense of organizing a series of doctrines ostensibly given in the Bible in accordance with an organizing principle (e.g. the so-called material principle of the Reformation). This presupposes that the Bible is a compendium of ready-made doctrines, sort of mixed up, like the pieces of a jigsaw puzzle, but if you discover the right principle, then you can arrange them in proper order. With the Erlangen theology this emphasizes the necessity of organic wholeness, but it does not break sufficiently with the notion of a rational system that is in accord with some universal principle.

16. Therefore: by a "system of theology" is meant a consistent understanding of the gospel, and a working out of all its implications. It is a matter of beginning at the center and then allowing that really to be determinative, and to radiate in every direction and permeate every detail. It is a matter of the "dominant motif."

In the light of what has been said, I trust this is clear. It is essentially Luther's "Was Christum treibt." It is the qualitative organic wholeness of which we have spoken. You cannot have a patchwork of opinion. There must be a consistent point of view which puts everything else in proper perspective.

Now at last we come to our problem:

17. Unity of faith must find expression in a "system of Theology" thus defined. It is not a matter of pious feeling but of precise doctrinal expressions and formulations which reveal clearly the basic

understanding of the gospel and of how the God relationship is established and maintained. At any given time men must discover whether or not they agree in the fashion described. Pious feeling is not enough. Everything depends upon the "system of theology" a man holds, be he peasant or king, illiterate or scholar.

So to repeat what has already been implied:

18. Unity of faith is not to be achieved by agreement upon one doctrinal system, fixated for all times in precisely those terms. This would be a human achievement, and would be a denial of the doctrine of justification by faith. It would mean controlling God by means of these doctrinal formulations. What I mean is simply that it would be a simple matter for us to set up a system of doctrine and then force everyone into this Procrustes' bed. This leads to inquisitions and to loveless fanaticism. Then we are at the controls, and we prescribe to men what they shall believe, instead of constantly listening to God's word.

We must, therefore, say it differently:

19. Unity of faith must in each generation become apparent as men wrestle with God to hear and understand what it is He has to say to them. Whether or not they are actually one in faith will become apparent to men as they work out all the implications of their understanding of the gospel in the contemporary situation. If I may speak somewhat as an outsider, I think it became quite clear in the conflict with Nazi tyranny how much unity of faith there was. This is how the problem must always solve itself anew, in the actual conflict. Now that the situation has changed, an apparent unity turns out to be none at all. So the conflict goes on, and what unity there is among us will become clear in the struggle. If some refuse to baptize infants, it is clear that there is no unity, and if some insist upon an episcopal succession we must go our separate ways.

20. So also the creeds and confessions of the past are to be understood as testimonies to real unity of faith. Understood in their historical context, the Lutheran confessional books will distinguish a total understanding of the gospel as over against alternatives (the "Schwärmer"—the Roman Catholics). What unites us as Lutherans today, therefore, is precisely the stand we take on those issues which are as alive and burning today as they ever were.

This is the problem of confessional subscription—whether or not the confessions are valid only as historical witnesses or have some kind of permanent significance. I am suggesting that, understood in their historical context, they have a permanent significance. Today we must still take our stand on the issues which confronted them, and which are still alive and burning today. Perhaps we can find an orientation that will provide a common vantage point from which the issues can be overcome, but in the meantime the same issues still divide us and we must choose where we will stand.

So we may now perhaps draw the conclusion:

21. The *satis est* of article VII is, therefore, not a hundred percent quantitative agreement upon an aggregate of separate doctrines, but means full agreement on a certain understanding of the gospel and of how the God relationship is established and maintained.

22. For this understanding of the gospel, the Bible is the *norma normans*, and the Confessions are the *norma normata*, because they set forth an understanding of the gospel believed to be in harmony with the Bible. And until it can be shown that they are not, this confession will continue to unite us as Lutherans.

23. If agreement on the gospel is essential to true unity of faith, this points the proper direction (Article VII). Oneness of organization, or the use of the same liturgy, or acceptance of certain formulas of confession, while allowing differences of opinion can never be primary. The position of the Augsburg Confession, which demands agreement in the understanding of the gospel while allowing differences in human rights and ceremonies, must not be reversed.

And now in conclusion a few random observations. What has been said is not to preclude the freedom to express the central understanding of the gospel in a variety of ways. Even as addressed to the same situation two men, who hold the same confession, may, nevertheless, choose to express themselves differently, and yet say the same thing. There may be different approaches and different emphases and different personal predilections. We are not all poured from the same mould.

Furthermore, there are some matters which really are adiaphora. There can be a variety of liturgies; there need not be the same form of church organization everywhere.

We must also make a distinction between opinions held by someone in private and those expressed publicly and as a teacher or preacher of the church. There are still areas of speculation. A man must also have the freedom to explore, and go where the winds of God carry him. There are the lonely souls, too, who are the correctives, who do not walk the beaten paths. To them we must listen. The church simply cannot be contained within any kind of man-made institution or be straight jacketed by man-made thoughts.

What has now been presented has been for the most part purely formal. There has not been much indication of what the actual content of the gospel is. Perhaps it was the intention that it was that content on which our attention should be focused. For me it can still be summarized in that *articulus stantis et cadentis ecclesiae,* justification by grace alone, for Christ's sake, through faith; but then this article must be understood in the dynamic way in which Luther understood it, and there must be freedom to apply it to our situation today. In the words of Luther: The true treasure of the church is the gospel of the glory and the grace of God. This treasure we possess in earthen vessels, and we must not confuse the vessels with the treasure.

In America the lines cut across the denominations, and one often finds a much better understanding of Luther among others than among fellow Lutherans. Perhaps it was always so; for it is a matter of understanding the gospel, and Lutherans have no monopoly of that. Nevertheless, the circumstances of history and perhaps God's governance, have put us where we are, and here we must bear our witness until God gives us the unity for which we yearn.

The Nature and Goal of Church Unity

By Prof. T. A. Kantonen

THE PRESENT DISCUSSION of the unity of the church seeks to consider: (1) unity as an essential ingredient in the concept of the church, (2) the nature of the unity to be sought in the effort to translate the concept into fact.

The Essential Unity

On the basis of the gospel we must begin with the fact that the unity of the church is a creation of the Holy Spirit, not a human construct. To the knowledge of faith it is not a dream or a hope but an accomplished fact. "By one Spirit we were all baptized into one body" (1 Cor. 12:13). The Spirit is one, not many, and the body of Christ, like Christ himself, is one, not many. The act of becoming a Christian is in itself incorporation into the new redeemed humanity whose head is Christ. In bestowing the gift of faith the Spirit creates fellowship with Christ and with all the members of His body. It is of the essence of the gospel that the *Gabe* always precedes the *Aufgabe*. What we are to do depends on what has already been given to us.

Over against artificial ecumenicity, evangelical theology must bear witness that the unity of the church bears the distinctive mark of the Spirit when it is seen to be a divine gift rather than a human achievement.

From this starting point we are led to emphasize, on the one hand, that what the Spirit creates is *koinonia,* fellowship, and, on the other hand, that the center of this fellowship is Christ.

Unity obtains a unique significance when *koinonia* is recognized as belonging to the essence of the church. The New Testament knows no such person as an isolated Christian. The Spirit who generates faith is the *vinculum* who binds believers to Christ and to one another. Just as sin divides mankind and sets brother against brother, so the forgiveness of sins in Christ unites men into the fellowship of the redeemed, which is the church. The communal idea is predominant in the Pauline metaphors in which the nature of the church is so powerfully dramatized. Thus in the basic metaphor of the body, individual believers are regarded as members, each having some special work, and grace with which to do it, but the emphasis is on their working together in mutual dependence and harmony. By incorporating them in Christ to share His cross and the power of His resurrection, the Spirit transforms them from a mere aggregation into a living organism.

The essence of the church as *koinonia* determines every phase of its thought and activity. Christian truth and Christian fellowship are inseparable. Christian ideas are not the same when they are uprooted from the soil of the fellowship. They have their vitality only as functionings of the living body of Christ. The same is true of the sacraments. Baptism and the Lord's Supper both presuppose the body of Christ into which we are incorporated, and in which we are nourished and sustained. The various offices of the church originate as differentiated functions of the one common life. Christian standards of conduct likewise presuppose the resources of the fellowship, and *agape* is the distinctive trait and the highest fruit of life in the Spirit.

Primary importance must, therefore, be ascribed to the communal character of the life created by the Spirit. True ecumenicity must be regarded as an essential trait of the church. But, as a creation of the Spirit, the church is by its nature a spiritual reality, and all external forms and structures are secondary in importance. What the Spirit creates, fellowship as well as faith, is essentially inward. It may have a variety of outward manifestations, but none of these can be given constitutive significance. The apostolic message stresses "unity of the

Spirit in the bond of peace," but the emergence of definite ecclesiastical order and the crystallization of specific ways of worship belong to history and tradition, not to the gospel itself. The original conception of the nature of the church's unity reappears clearly in Luther: "The essence, life, and nature of Christendom is not a bodily assembly but an assembly of hearts in one faith. . . . It is a spiritual unity, on account of which men are called the communion of saints. And this unity is of itself enough to constitute Christendom, and without it no unity, be it of place, of time, of person, of work, or of whatever else, makes Christendom. . . . The real, true, essential Christendom is a spiritual thing, and not anything external or outward" (W. A. 6, 293, 296). In modern language this means that the unity of the church is fundamentally a matter of function rather than of structure. The church as the one indivisible body of Christ exists wherever the gospel is being proclaimed and the Holy Spirit through it generates faith. The mission for which the Spirit uses the fellowship implies proclaimers and hearers, time and place, all the manifold means and structures of organized activity. But the evangelical view of the church is irreconcilable with any position which makes an external rite, form, tradition, or institution a constitutive element in the church.

The affirmation that the unity of the church is to be found in the fellowship created by the Spirit leads to an equally strong affirmation that the center around which the Spirit integrates the church is Christ. In the redeeming strategy of God the work of Christ is the foundation of the work of the Spirit. The Spirit does not speak about himself but about Christ, nor does He lead men to himself but to Christ. He takes that which is Christ's and communicates it to Christ's people. He teaches and imparts the mind of Christ. He does not reveal God in general, or God in the abstract, but God in Christ. He makes the God who became incarnate in Christ a personally experienced reality to men of every age. From the point of view of the life of the church, no meaningful distinction can be made between Christ and the Spirit. "The Lord is the Spirit" (2 Cor. 3:17). Without Christ we do not have the Spirit, and without the Spirit we do not have Christ. This emphasis on the intimate relation between the Spirit, the creator of unity, and Christ, the center of unity, serves a twofold purpose. On the one hand, it exposes the superficiality of unification based on mere "religious" or "spiritual" interests which men have in common. The Spirit who works through the Christ-centered Word to lead men to a personal commitment to Christ is not concerned with harmonizing men's spirituality or promoting institu-

[39]

tional efficiency but in creating and vitalizing a "communion of saints," i.e., in binding the hearts of believers to their Lord and to one another. On the other hand, it prevents an inadequate conception of Christ as a mere historical figure, whose teachings we are asked to accept and whose example we are asked to follow. Our "unity in Christ" becomes more than a figure of speech when the Spirit mediates to us the power of His resurrection and the fullness of His grace.

The proper acknowledgment of the Christological foundation of the church provides the perspective for seeing the church in its relation to the kingdom of God and to divine revelation as a whole. It is the Messianic community, the instrument through which God fulfils His purpose for mankind. It is "the Israel of God" (Gal. 6:16), "Abraham's offspring, heirs according to promise" (Gal. 3:29), "the true circumcision" (Phil. 3:3). The Messiah's life, death, and resurrection ushered in the new age in which the New Covenant is realized. For those who are "in Christ" the Messianic age has already begun. The risen Christ has brought into the present world the life of the world to come, and the Spirit provides access to this life. The church is the firstfruits of the new aeon, the colony of heaven on earth. It looks to the future for the final consummation of the kingdom, but in giving His people the "earnest" *(arrabon)* of His Spirit, God has already given an initial installment of the coming kingdom. Heavenly power is therefore manifest here and now in the heirs of the kingdom. They have been redeemed from the dominion of darkness and transferred into the kingdom of the Son of God's love. When the church sees its existence and mission in this perspective, it discovers its unity in the depths of God's eternal purpose in Christ.

The Unity to Be Sought

In view of the foregoing analysis, the existing state of disunity among the churches should give us grave concern. It appears to be nothing less than a sin against the Lord of the church and a denial of the very essence of the church. It is the nature of sin to divide, and of the Spirit to create fellowship. Christians have become so accustomed to the inertia of following the old grooves, and of stressing the points in which they differ, that they have lost the consciousness of guilt that should accompany reflection on the divided state of the church. It is possible for an infidel sociologist or historian to analyze the situation with cool and detached academic objectivity. A sincere Christian can approach it only with deep heart searching and penitence.

The state of disunity is deplorable not only from the general Christian point of view, but also from the specific point of view of historic Lutheranism. The schismatic spirit which gives rise to numberless sects, each arrogantly clinging to its own ideology and condemning others, is foreign to authentic Lutheranism. The spirit of our Confessions is remarkably broad, constructive, and conciliatory. The aim is not to show how many obstacles stand in the way of unity, but how few. "To the true unity of the Church it is enough to agree concerning the doctrine of the Gospel and the administration of the sacraments. Nor is it necessary that human traditions, rites, or ceremonies, instituted by men, should be everywhere alike" (Augs. Conf. VII). The Church of Christ is, therefore, affirmed to exist beyond the adherents of the Confessions themselves, for it embraces "men scattered throughout the whole world, from the rising to the setting of the sun, who agree concerning the gospel, and have the same Christ, the same Holy Ghost, and the same sacraments, no matter whether they have human traditions that are the same or dissimilar" (Apol. VII, Conc. Trigl. p. 229). The condemnations in the Confessions are directed, as the Preface to the Formula of Concord explicitly states, not against "entire churches, which are either under the Roman Empire of the German nation, or elsewhere; nay, rather it has been our purpose and disposition, in this manner, openly to censure and condemn only the fanatical opinions and their obstinate and blasphemous teachers."

According to the classical Lutheran position, then, the nature of the unity we seek is unity in the confession of the same faith, the faith that is generated by the Holy Spirit through the gospel. In the expression that the basis of unity is agreement on "the doctrine of the gospel" the emphasis is upon the *gospel* rather than upon *doctrine*. Only the gospel is important but it is all-important. As Luther said in commenting on the apostolic succession, which even today is of such constitutive importance to some churches, "the Gospel has to be the successio" (W. A. 39, II, 177). The gospel to Luther was synonymous with the Word of God, God's dynamic communication of himself to us in Christ, which, he said, constitutes the whole life and substance of the church. He defined the Word of God as "the Gospel of God concerning his Son." Where the gospel is proclaimed and taught, there the living Christ himself confronts men, there faith, as a personal wholehearted commitment to Christ, *takes place*, there the Holy Spirit unites men into that "assembly of hearts in one faith" which is the essence of the church.

The doctrine of the gospel is simply the attempt to express the meaning of the gospel. It is the consummation of faith in the realm of thought. The doctrine of the gospel has the same relation to the gospel as a philosophy of life has to life itself. The way to unity by way of doctrinal agreement is the effort to reach a common understanding of the faith we live by. It is the effort to mean the same thing when we speak about Christ, His gospel, and His church. Only one who is indifferent to truth can deny the importance of such an effort. But this way is beset with many difficulties. We know in part and we prophesy in part. Ecumenical conversation often reminds one of the blind men of Hindustan, each of whom touched a different part of an elephant and proceeded to argue vehemently, on the basis of knowledge that was both empirical and existential, that the elephant is like a rope, or a tree, or a wall. I believe that we can safely prophesy that the time will never come when all denominations will accept all the teachings of all the other denominations. In fact, Christian faith at its most vital level is such an intensely personal matter that complete objective unanimity is quite impossible even within the same denomination. Already during the Reformation people laughed at the story of two Thuringian peasants who came to blows because one was a follower of Martin, the other of Luther. Even professional theologians, supposedly wiser and more synoptic, are not exempt from this predicament. If the unity of the church had to wait until theologians came to full agreement, we would wait forever. The spectacle of *"rabies theologorum,"* theologians foaming at the mouth as they castigate one another, led an undenominational liberal, Walther Köhler, a disciple of Troeltsch, to say that dogmatics is not Christianity, but only the dead and poisonous slag that Christianity leaves along its path.

From the point of view of the doctrine of the gospel, however, no such contrast can be drawn between Christianity and theology. I recall an occasion many years ago when I heard Karl Heim lecture to a group of pastors on the Christian message for our day. In the discussion following the lecture one of the pastors asked, "Should our emphasis today be on Christian life or on Christian doctrine?" Heim's reply was, "A question like that should never be asked. This is not an either-or. Our emphasis should be neither on life nor on doctrine but on living doctrine." That is what the gospel is, living doctrine. It is not a set of static propositions to which we are asked to subscribe. It is kerygma, living message, witness, the power of God which the church is commissioned to release into the lives of all men. The demand for unity in the doctrine of the gospel is the demand that the witness be clear and strong, that the trumpet give not an uncertain sound.

The New Testament shows a singular disregard for the church in its organizational and institutional aspect. The question whether Jesus founded a church at all in the sense of an institution will remain forever debatable. His prayer for the unity of His people was in the context "that they may know thee, the only true God" and "that they may be consecrated in truth." But this unifying truth is nothing abstract or speculative. It centers in Him who is the truth, and who gives men new life in faith. Hence the Lord prays "that they may all be one . . . so that the world may believe." The necessity of bearing united witness to the world is indeed the impelling motive behind the ecumenical movement of our day, and ecumenicity is inseparably connected with the missionary enterprise. Since the church, as Emil Brunner puts it, exists by mission just as fire exists by burning, and since the mission of the church is to preach the gospel to every creature, it is of utmost importance that the proclamation of the church is the true Gospel of Christ. Luther goes so far as to say that false teaching which obscures the forgiveness of sins in Christ is worse than sin itself. This was also the apostolic emphasis. Recall the uncompromising stand which Paul took against those who substituted a Jewish legalism for the gospel of free grace. "If an angel from heaven should preach to you a gospel contrary to that which we preached to you, let him be accursed" (Gal. 1: 8). The attitude in 1 John toward the speculation of the Gnostics who denied the reality of the incarnation is just as firm: "Every spirit which confesses that Jesus Christ has come in the flesh is of God, and every spirit which does not confess Jesus is not of God. This is the spirit of antichrist" (4: 2-3). The apostles were not willing to sacrifice the purity of the gospel to the will to stay together.

The unity we seek is "the unity of the Spirit in the bond of peace," with "one hope, one Lord, one faith, one baptism, one God and Father of us all" (Eph. 4: 3-6). But having affirmed this, we have not solved our problem but only taken the first step on the road to the solution. The questions still remain: what spirit? what hope? what lord? what faith? We may say, "We want no creed but the New Testament," but it does not mean much so long as there are so many interpretations of the New Testament. One of the study pamphlets prepared for Evanston stated that to many people in the pews John 3: 16 means: "God once inspired a certain Jew to tell his contemporaries that there is much to be said for loving one another." When we try to put into words the profounder meaning of the New Testament message, we are on our way to formulating a creed. Creeds are inescapable. As Emerson said of Brahma, "When me they fly I am the wings." The earliest New Testament creed is Peter's confession, "Thou art the Christ, the Son of the living God," simplified by the apostolic Church into the words "Jesus is Lord." All the confessions of the early church have this same basic Christological motivation. It is not enough to say, "We all believe in Christ; let us therefore all be one." The fathers at Nicea literally tore to pieces an Arian creed that made Christ something less than "very God of very God." That is the kind of situation that the Jesuit Father Pribilla had in mind in replying to Archbishop Söderblom's remark, "What is it that unites us? We answer: discipleship of Christ." "But how," asked Pribilla, "can we be united in discipleship of Christ if we are not agreed as to who Christ is?"

The ecumenical movement today is determined to meet that challenge. We have discovered, as Bishop Nygren expresses it, that "the way to the center is the way to unity." Instead of an artificial and superficial readjustment of externals, we are striving for unity by a deepening at the point of centrality. It is encouraging that the Edinburgh Conference on Faith and Order in 1937, which could not fully agree on anything else, did adopt unanimously the report on the basic doctrine of the grace of our Lord Jesus Christ. The real turning point came in 1952 when the Lund Conference set up a long-range program to study the nature of the church in its relation to the doctrine of Christ and of the Holy Spirit. In one respect, however, Lund took a step backward instead of forward. The Lausanne Conference in 1927 had agreed to make the early ecumenical creeds the basis for future discussion. The statement on "consensus in doctrine" in the Lund report expresses only a variety of conflicting opinions: "All accept the Holy Scriptures as either the sole authority for doctrine or the primary and decisive part of those authorities to which they would appeal. Most accept the Ecumenical Creeds as an interpretation of the truth of the Bible, or as marking a distinctive stage in the working out of the orthodox faith. Some assign a special importance to the creedal documents of the early Ecumenical Councils. Some would say that to found unity on any creeds is to found it on something human, namely, our understanding of the gospel and our theological work in formulating its meaning. Some judge in accordance with the Inner Light and the leadings of the Spirit, and are, therefore, concerned to witness against the use of outward creeds when these are held to be necessary or sufficient."

True living unity cannot be achieved, of course, by a mere acceptance and repetition of formulas, either ancient or modern. But it is both unwarranted and shortsighted to set the spontaneous expressions of faith today in opposition to the historic creeds of Christendom. The Apostles' Creed and the Nicene Creed ought to be as inspiring to every Christian as the Te Deum and perhaps ought to be sung rather than recited in order to furnish their full inspiration. The confessions of the past are not shackles that bind us. They are heart-throbs of the faith of the fathers. They are coalbeds in which the light and energy of vital Christian witness have been preserved. It is for us to release this energy for our own use so that our faith may be positive and strong Christian faith. Not only must we have this vital continuity with the whole communion of saints which death itself cannot sever, but the theology being forged in current ecumenical conversation must also become confessional theology. It must be more than theological reports. It must be clear common witness of the Lord who unites us and, like the ancient confessions, it must find its way into the worship and thought and life of the congregations to produce that unity which comes from consecration in truth.

We must love one another, yes, but in love we must also speak the truth to one another as God gives us to see the truth. Our unity must be an honest unity, which does not compromise or override mind and conscience. The nature of the unity we seek is determined by our understanding of the nature of Christ and of His Church. If it is the purpose of Christ to organize into a world-wide institution all those who are willing to bear the name Christian, then we should give to the ecclesiastical architects and engineers the task of dismantling the present denominational structures, of constructing a streamlined super church, at least of piecing together some kind of mosaic, without too much regard for existing disagreement in matters of faith. But if the church is the community of those whom the Holy Spirit has united with Christ, then the primary concern is organic unity with Christ, not organizational mechanics. Then a wholehearted response to the living Christ, spiritual renewal through repentance and faith, and the consequent clearer and more consecrated witness are the basic prerequisites. It is to this profounder unity that the Lord is now leading His people as they are receptive to the Spirit who makes Christ a living reality, guides into all truth, and binds the hearts of believers together in love.

[45]

Ekklesia and Ekklesiai in the New Testament

By Prof. Karl Karner

1. Ἐκκλησία means *"assembly"* in the sense of "self-assembling" and also in the sense of a "deliberating and determining assembly." This meaning is still extant for the Greek-speaking primitive Christian congregations and for the New Testament, as witnessed to not only in Acts 19:32ff., but also throughout New Testament usage. Here, first and foremost, *ekklesia* is the concrete "congregation" assembled in divine service. On this basis it is understandable that Paul speaks of the *ekklesia* "of the Thessalonians" (1 Thess. 1:1) or "at Cenchreae" (Rom. 16:1) or of the ἡ κατ' οἶκον ἐκκλησία (Rom. 16:5), and that we also hear in the plural of the *ekklesiai* of Judea, Galatia, etc. (Gal. 1:22; 1:2). And since the *ekklesia* is an "assembly," it is "gathered" (Acts 15:30), "comes together" and "assembles itself" (1 Cor. 11:18; 14:23. Cf. Acts 11:26).

The *ekklesia* receives its distinctive individuality by means of additions which fix its limits over against other "profane" assemblies: it is the *ekklesia* "in God the Father and the Lord Jesus Christ" (1 Thess. 1:1; 2 Thess. 1:1) or "in Christ" (Gal. 1:22). However, it can also be used in the plural: αἱ ἐκκλησίαι τοῦ θεοῦ (1 Thess. 2:14; 2 Thess.

1:4; 1 Cor. 11:16) or τοῦ χριστοῦ (Rom. 16:16). The genitive use here indicates that the "assemblies" of God (or Christ) are placed under Him, belong to Him, and are ruled by Him. The coupling of this genitive with the plural of *ekklesia* affirms both that in the idea of the Word an additional element is perceptible, and also that the *ekklesia* has a steadfastness which reaches out beyond the time and space limitations of the worshiping assembly: it is a "congregation" and "church."

2a. In the New Testament, the "profane" word *ekklesia* is filled with a distinctive new content which has nothing to do with the general Greek usage of the word and, consequently, is not derived from it. It follows that the choice of this word for the primitive Christian worshiping "assemblies" is not to be understood from general Greek language usage. Rather, it points back to the Septuagint (cf. Acts 7:28; Hebr. 2:12); that is, back to the Old Testament content of the words in the Septuagint. The *ekklesia* is the extension and eschatological fulfillment or realization of the Old Testament *"kehal JHVH."* Because of this it is fundamentally ἐκκλησία τοῦ θεοῦ (1 Cor. 1:2 etc.): the summons and assembly of the (new) *People of God* whom God has elected and called. It is the "Israel of God" (Gal. 6:16): not as the unbroken extension of the "Israel after the flesh," but rather as built upon the "remnant chosen by grace" (Rom. 11:5), a "people of inheritance" (1 Pet. 2:9), called "not from the Jews only but also from the Gentiles" (Rom. 9:24).

2b. The *ekklesia* is *"a peculiar people"* (1 Pet. 2:9) and appears as such—to use the words of the apostle Paul—as the "body of Christ." For in the new people of God, Christ is the Lord: He rules as head of the body, building it through the Spirit into the "house of God" (Col. 2:19; Eph. 2:21), as the members are baptized into one body, serving the Lord and caring for one another in mutual love through the gifts of the Spirit (Rom. 12:11; 1 Cor. 12:25).

This must be supplemented at two points. In public worship—in the proclamation of the gospel, in the various gifts of the Spirit, and especially in Holy Communion—the *ekklesia* becomes palpably concrete as the body of Christ. Here Christ is present, and the congregation has communion (κοινωνία) with Him, as it partakes of His atoning death. The worshiping *ekklesia*, therefore, is not merely one among various forms in which the *ekklesia* lives its life or expresses itself. It is its peculiar mode of appearance. Hence, in Paul's language, the expressions, "to come together in the *ekklesia*," and "to come together at the same place" (συνέρχεσθαι ἐπὶ τὸ αὐτό) , in the sense of "to come together for divine service," are clearly synonymous (1 Cor. 11: 19-20).

To this we add a second consideration: the divine service in the sense of the θρησκεία and the cultic λειτουργίαι in which man brings something to God are taken over in the New Testament. Hence, these and other similar designations come forth very seldom in the New Testament, and then usually in a spiritualized sense; Christ himself is set forth by God as an "expiation" ἱλαστήριον (Rom. 3:25), and the ἐφάπαξ character of His atoning death renders unnecessary any form of material sacrifice as a divine service (Heb. 7:27; 9:11-14). Through baptism we are incorporated and buried into the death of Christ; through Holy Communion we share with the congregation in the gifts of His fulfilled reconciliation. Through these the congregation and all of its members are built into the "temple of God" (1 Cor. 3:16; 6:15-20). Yet, as the body of Christ, the *ekklesia* is not a "peculiar people" in a statically bound sense, but rather chosen "that ye should show forth the praises of him who hath called you out of darkness into his marvelous light" (1 Pet. 2:9). To the life and concrete reality of the *ekklesia* as the body of Christ belong not only the gift of its Lord in being built into the house of God, but also the "new life," the witness of God and His grace in Christ. It is just this new life that Paul calls the "spiritual divine service," "the living, holy, and God-pleasing sacrifice" (Rom. 12:1-3). Since the divine service as man's bringing of material sacrifices has been overcome in the reconciling death of Christ, the whole life of the Christian is incorporated into divine service.

The *ekklesia* assumes real, concrete presence on earth as Christ is present in the communion of saints (1 Cor. 14:33), in the "sacraments," in the proclamation of the Word and prophesy, and as He "lives" in all the individual members (Gal. 2:20). He creates the saints who are called from the Jews and Gentiles into new creatures (2 Cor. 5:17: Gal. 6:15), into new—eschatological—men (Eph. 2:15). This new humanity will also be revealed with Him in glory when Christ himself appears, who is its life (Col. 3:4).

3. The *ekklesia* of God appears in the congregation which is assembled at a time and place for worship. Yet it is not "partitioned" among the several *ekklesiai* or the total of all the single *ekklesiai*. Nor does it come about through the merger of the several *ekklesiai*. It is also misleading to say that, while the several *ekklesiai* are a unity in themselves—in the mission situation of the New Testament—yet in so far as they are the body of Christ, they must first become a

unity as an *ekklesia*.[1] For in each single concrete *ekklesia*, the whole
ekklesia of God is "present in its inseparable totality."[2]

This is derived, first of all, from the fact that the notion of the
"*kehal JHVH*" is incorporated within the Messianic efficacy of Jesus.
Jesus does not proclaim the kingdom of God to men in general. He
does not address His call for repentance to "*the*" people, but rather
to His people, and that means to the people of God. He knows himself
to be sent "to the lost sheep of the house of Israel" (Matt. 15:24). He
was brought to lament over the people who were weary and scattered
"like sheep without a shepherd" (Matt. 9:24; cf. Mark 6:34), and
wanted to "gather" precisely this people (Matt. 12:30, 25:32). He
has not come to be served, but rather to serve and to give His life as
a ransom for "many," for the people of God (Mark 10:45). According
to the account in the Gospels, on the night before His death, Jesus
designated His life given to death and His body and blood shed for
many as the sacrifice which would establish the new covenant between
God and His people. The eschatological new covenant and the people
of God—the "*kehal JHVH*"—belong together. It is, therefore, per-
fectly consistent that Peter's confession of the Messianic mission of
Jesus in Matt. 16:18 is answered by the word concerning the *ekklesia*
of Jesus, the people of God whom He has gathered.

At the same time it dare not be forgotten that Jesus did not merely
equate the people of God with the historically given people of "Israel
after the flesh." Already John the Baptist knew that God could raise
up children of Abraham from the stones instead of from that generation of vipers which boasted about the fatherhood of Abraham (Matt.
3:9). In like manner, Jesus preached not only judgment to the evil
and faithless generation against whom one day the people of Nineveh
would arise as witnesses (Matt. 12:39ff), but He also proclaimed that
repentant tax collectors and harlots would enter into the kingdom of
God before the "righteous" and pious (Matt. 21:31). Indeed, He saw
also many coming from east and west who will sit at table with the
Patriarchs in the kingdom of heaven (Matt. 8:11).

This new people of God, the ἐκκλησία τοῦ θεοῦ, which is established
by Jesus' death and resurrection and is gathered through the eschatological gift of the Spirit, is given over to the single concrete
ekklesia. In the concrete *ekklesia* the people of God makes its appearance. Paul can, therefore, speak of the *ekklesia* of God "which is
in Corinth" (1 Cor. 1:2). From this perspective it is also understandable why one may use *ekklesia* in either the single or the plural without any perceivable difference (Gal. 1:13,22; 1 Cor. 11:16,18,22). Nor

[50]

are any differences to be noted in the place-and-time-bounded *ekklesiai* "in Christ." The original congregation in Jerusalem is just as much *ekklesia* as is the congregation in Antioch (cf. Acts 11:22,26). The "local congregations" are not merely offshoots of the *ekklesia* in Jerusalem, but rather in each of them the same ἐκκλησία τοῦ θεοῦ is present "in undivided wholeness."

4. To the distinguishing characteristics peculiar to the *ekklesia* of God belong *oneness, unity,* and *unanimity.*

a) The *oneness* of the *ekklesia* results from the fact that it is the *one* people of God redeemed through the *one* Christ. Christ is the "second Adam," the beginner of a new humanity in which God has reconciled himself with the world. He is the One who has died for us all (2 Cor. 5:14ff.). Jesus Christ, the only begotten Son is the one and only Lord (1 Cor. 8:6) whom God has exalted and given a name which is above all names (Phil. 2:9), and therefore "there is salvation in no one else" (Acts 4:12). In baptism we are baptized into His death so that we might walk in newness of life. In Holy Communion we partake of Him, for the blessed chalice is the "community" of His blood; that is, we participate in the life which He has given for us. Partaking of the bread broken in Holy Communion is likewise "community," a sharing in the body of Christ (1 Cor. 10:16ff.). So it is Christ who is made our righteousness: by faith we are justified. Therefore Christ—as its "head"—"gathers" the Church of God (John 11:52), His body, through the "sacraments" and the Word of reconciliation of the new people of God.

The "body of Christ" is the *ekklesia* in a double sense. Those who have been engrafted in baptism and grafted by the Spirit into the *ekklesia* are "members" of the "body" who perform their tasks as bodily functions. In like manner, Christ is the "head" of the *ekklesia,* not only as its commanding Lord, but also as He who holds together the whole body and grants its growth so that the *ekklesia* is built in Spirit into *one* House of God (Col. 2:19; Eph. 2:21).

The one and only atonement corresponds to the one and only *ekklesia,* the body of Christ. This is the "fullness," the congregation fulfilled by Christ—or more correctly, perhaps, in Patristic and Reformation exegesis—the complementing (*complementum*) or completion of "the fullness of him who fills all in all" (Eph. 1:23). The one Christ rules in his body as κεφαλὴ ὑπὲρ πάντα, supplying all His members with His Spirit and working in them a godly life. Consequently, the *ekklesia* is an "*ekklesia* of saints" (1 Cor. 14:33).

b) Belonging inseparably together in the New Testament are

the one and only Christ, the sole foundation of His *ekklesia* (1 Cor. 3:11), and the one and only *ekklesia* of God as the people of God and as the body of Christ. They are seen neither as members of the same grade nor as co-ordinated one with another, but are presented rather as head and body. In His body, by "Word" and "sacrament," Christ makes His completed redemption efficacious and contemporary. The *ekklesia* is the body of Christ, in so far as Christ is *praesens* in it.

Christ works through His Spirit in the *ekklesia*. This is one and the same Spirit despite the diversity of its gifts (1 Cor. 12:4ff.). Through this one Spirit are all Christians baptized into one body (1 Cor. 12:13). The Holy Communion is also πνευματικὸν βρῶμα and πόμα (cf. 1 Cor. 10:3-4). The Spirit speaks in the proclamation of the Word and prophesy. Indeed, the resurrected, glorified, and reigning Lord of the *ekklesia* is himself the Spirit (2 Cor. 3:17).

Faith as the new form of the God relationship, hope as the witness to the new existence in Christ, love both to God and in service to the neighbor, peace and joy as eschatological gifts of salvation: these are all the presents of the Spirit of the Lord of the *ekklesia*. The one faith and the one hope are enjoined—as is the one *ekklesia*—to the one body of Christ, along with the one Spirit, the one Lord and the one God and Father (Eph. 4:4-6). Therefore there is only one gospel (Gal. 1:6-7), the one and only power of God, through which God in Christ justifies the sinner.

It is in the *ekklesia* that the risen and glorified Christ, the Lord on earth, lives and works. Here He gives himself to His own, forgives sin, becomes our justification, sanctification, and redemption (1 Cor. 1:30). As the body of Christ, this *ekklesia* is His function.

c) As Christ with all His gifts of salvation is still the indivisible One (cf. 1 Cor. 1:16), so too *unity* is a fundamental characteristic of the *ekklesia*. Through Adam's Fall, "death spread to all men because all men sinned." In like manner—indeed, to an even still higher degree—the obedience and "just act" of the one Christ work themselves out (Rom. 5:12ff.). It is one people which stands together in the discipleship of Christ. It is one body—to be sure, with many members and functions according to the different gifts of the Spirit — but still one body which "grows into a holy temple in the Lord" (Eph. 2:21), and serves the Lord in holy love (Rom. 12:11). It is a new, eschatological people of God, Jew and Gentile *alike*, called and created out of both "to a new humanity" which is reconciled to God "in *one* body through the cross" (Eph. 2:14ff.).

Therefore neither circumcision nor uncircumcision mean anything in the *ekklesia,* but only the new creature (Gal. 6:15). Such differences are here overtaken and overcome which otherwise separate men from each other. All are God's children through faith in Christ Jesus, all are "one in Christ Jesus" (Gal. 3:26-28). The *ekklesia* is "one flock" which has "one shepherd" (John 10:16). The unity of the *ekklesia* is grounded in the relationship to its Lord: the *ekklesia* is one with the Son, as the Son is one with the Father (John 17:23).

Above all, the unity of the church is given as κοινωνία in a two-fold sense. First, it is a "community" (κοινωνία is *communio* with Christ); that is, participating in the body and blood of Christ (1 Cor. 10:16) and, in this sense, it is a "sacramental community." On the other hand, the *ekklesia* is simultaneously a "community" (κοινωνία) of its members with one another. Through mutual work in the building of the *ekklesia,* its members are bound inseparably to each other, sharing their joys and sorrows together (1 Cor. 12:26; Rom. 12:15). They maintain "the unity of the Spirit in the bond of peace" (Eph. 4:3).

d) The unity of the *ekklesia* must work itself out as *unanimity.* The community of the *ekklesia* comes to expression in common confession of the one Lord (1 Cor. 12:3; Rom. 10:9). The unanimity of the church is in "the community of confession," in the sense that through the confession Christ is proclaimed. In proclamation and "doctrine," the word of reconciliation is inseparable from confession and the *ekklesia* itself. The *ekklesia* practices the "service of reconciliation" in which apostles, prophets, teachers, and various other renderings of service are ordained by God (1 Cor. 12:28; cf. Eph. 4:11).

In this community of sacrament and confession—and in the Word's proclamation with its accompanying "office"— the one *ekklesia* of the living God testifies to itself as "the pillar and bulwark of the truth" (1 Tim. 3:15).

In Christ, His service, and His gifts, the unity and unanimity of the *ekklesia* come to reality, at the same time as they remain its task and goal in the continual striving for holiness (Eph. 5:25-27). Therefore Christ prays for His disciples "that they may all be one;" indeed, ἵνα ὦσιν τετελειωμένοι εἰσ ἕν (John 17:21-23). The inner unanimity of the *ekklesia* is endangered from the very outset by sin, dissension, divisions, and by "doctrines" deviating from the gospel (cf. the "mission situation" of the Apostolic Church in 1 Cor. 5:1ff., 1:10ff., 3:1ff. as well as among the Galatians). "If the unity of the body of Christ ... is to come into appearance, it also requires polemical marks."[3] For this reason, special importance is to be attached to the various apostolic exhortations for struggle against the "works of the flesh," in favor of concord and holiness. They are not only moral admonitions for the congregation and individual Christians, but are also Christologically and ecclesiologically determined.

5. The New Testament *ekklesia* is no smoothed out and uniform mass, but is rather a living body with its members performing differing services. These services also condition the *differences* in the *ekklesia*. In Christ, to be sure, the differences among men brought about by the Fall are overcome. Out of Jews and Gentiles, a new people of God has come forth in Christ. Nevertheless, differences remain in the *ekklesia*. The *ekklesia* in Jerusalem holds fast to the law; indeed, its members are "zealous for the law" (Acts 21:20). Occasionally we hear that some of the Christians in Jerusalem have taken upon themselves a Nazarite vow (Acts 21:23-26). On the other hand, the congregations which have been founded through the mission of St. Paul hold neither the circumcision nor dietary laws, and they offer no sacrificial gifts in the temple of Jerusalem. They are "freed from the law," "dead to the law through the body of Christ" (Rom. 7:4-6). Paul admonishes the Galatians to remain in the "liberty" to which Christ has freed them (Gal. 5:1).

We know of differences extant within the several "local congregations" as well. In Rome there were differences between the "strong" and the "weak" regarding certain foods and fasting. The severance from paganism did not proceed uniformly in the several congregations, as shown by the Epistle to the Corinthians in the Pauline congregations and by the Book of Revelation (Ch. 2-3) in the Near East congregations. In addition must also be cited various Jewish, heathen, and Gnostic influences which contributed to differences in both thought and action among their adherents.

These differences, however, did not destroy the *koinonia* between Jewish and Gentile Christians, groups and "parties," "strong" and "weak," Palestinian and Pauline *ekklesiai*. To be sure, under certain circumstances the "differences" between or within congregations endangered the unity and *koinonia* as evidenced in the Galatian congregations or in the Corinthian congregation as plagued with "factional struggles" and divisions. And though the αἱρέσεις (1 Cor. 11:18ff.) had not broken the unity of the *ekklesia* at the time of the writing of 1 Corinthians, still *ekklesia* and αἱρέσεις were seen as mutually exclusive. The αἵρεσις is seen as a "work of the flesh" (Gal. 5:20), "false heresy" wrongly brought in by "false prophets" (cf. 2 Pet. 2:1) as an eschatological reality and danger for the unity of the congregation.

Therefore differences and oppositions in the congregation must be purified and divisions reconciled. Under these circumstances, the apostolic admonitions to concord and mutual toleration of both the weak and the strong in the faith take on special importance. Paul never writes to the Corinthians or Galatians about the abrogation of the community; for that he gives no direction. Nor are there any allusions as to how, or under what circumstances, a severed community could be reunited again.

The "controversy" over circumcision (Acts 15), and the struggle of the apostle with the Galatians, concerned not only the *koinonia* between Jewish and Gentile Christians, but also the whole question of law observance by the Gentile Christians. As Paul expressed it, the gospel itself was at stake. The accounts in Acts and Galatians agree that the resolution of the questions in controversy would not take place by theological utterances or through the formulation of a valid and mutually recognized "doctrine" of the law. Rather, accord was to be reached by the recognition of the witnesses of God which the Spirit also gave to the Gentiles (Acts 15:8); that is, through the recognition that Paul had been entrusted with the "gospel to the uncircumcised" (Gal. 2:7). The *koinonia* between the members of the congregations and the congregations one with another does not come about through human deliberations or agreements, but rather through the work of God in Christ and through the work and gifts of the Holy Spirit. In like manner, the endangered *koinonia* is not saved by theological presentations and agreement on a rigid "doctrine," but rather through obedience to the divine witness. Paul also fought against those who were "perverting" the Galatian congregations, both by his proclamation of justification by faith and by his pointing out the freedom given in the Spirit. Through Christ, the liberation from bondage has actually taken place, and the life in the Spirit testifies to the reality of this freedom.

Even if they are a product of a later reformulation, the events reported in Acts 15—like the Galatian struggle—are illustrative for the whole New Testament. In substance they repeat themselves in the struggles against "heresy," as for example, in Colossians and in the later New Testament writings. In the Pastoral Epistles, stress is laid upon the meaning and necessity of "sound doctrine" (1 Tim. 1:10) as over against the spreading of "different doctrine" (1 Tim. 1:3, 6:3) and the "profane old wives' tales" (1 Tim. 4:7). It is the "preacher, apostle, and teacher" himself (2 Tim. 1:11) who impresses upon his co-workers in varying ways that they are to be diligent in teaching and to give attention to "doctrine." But "doctrine" here is not yet the dogmatic fixation and formulation of instruction *about* the "truths" of the gospel. It is rather the proclamation of the "mystery of godliness" (1 Tim 3:16) that is, the revelation itself which occurred in Christ. This "doctrine" is "sound" because it witnesses to the revelation in Christ of the "saving grace of God" and thereby leads to deliverance.

6. Just as James, Cephas, and John gave to the Apostle Paul and to Barnabas the "right hand of fellowship" (κοινωνία, Gal. 2:9), so, too, the local congregations shared "community" among each other. Fundamental was the "community" within the several congregations themselves. κοινωνία is oneness in heart and soul and spiritual unity (cf. Acts 4:32), as well as sharing in the Holy Ghost (2 Cor. 13:13), and responsiveness to the poor among the saints in Jerusalem (Rom. 15:26). Deepest, however, is the "vertical" and "horizontal" *community in Holy Communion.*

The κοινωνία was fostered between the several *ekklesiai* as well as within them. The Book of Acts reports that Peter and John visited the congregation in Samaria on behalf of the Jerusalem congregation with which the Antioch group was in lively contact. Paul also nurtured the *koinonia* with the Jerusalem congregation. From Gal. 2:11ff. we know that the *koinonia* between the congregations included sacramental fellowship, the care and stability of which was sometimes endangered so that the mingling of the Jewish and Gentile Christians had to be regulated. Although the New Testament gives us no special account of the fostering of Holy Communion fellowship among the congregations, it may be said on the basis of Gal. 2:11ff. that this practice was taken as self-evident. In the New Testament we hear of no cases in which sacramental fellowship would be abrogated. To be sure, cases such as those of the Corinthian incestuous sinner (1 Cor. 5:1ff.), and the apostasy, i.e. excommuncation of Hymenaeus, Alexander, and then Philetus (1 Tim. 1:20; 2 Tim. 2:17) demand, of course, that sacramental fellowship be broken. Perhaps it is also witnessed to in the case of Diotrephes (3 John 9-11), by the renunciation of a congregational leader ("bishop"?), and the part of the congregation loyal to church fellowship. This renunciation presumably meant also a breach in the sacramental fellowship.

From the beginning, fellowship among the congregations in Holy Communion was exclusive. But the boundaries of exclusiveness were not drawn between the congregations themselves, but over against the "world." For the Pauline congregations, the person of the apostle himself provided a unifying power for the congregations also in regard to sacramental fellowship (cf. Acts 20: 5-7). That brothers from without had to prove that they belonged to the *ekklesia* by confessing the διδαχὴ τοῦ χριστοῦ is testified to already in 2 John 9-10. Indeed, all the *ekklesiai* of the whole world are *one* ἀδελφότης (1 Pet. 2: 17, 5: 9).

This also shows that the *ekklesiai* of the New Testament are one ἐκκλησία τοῦ θεοῦ.

Notes

[1] Cf. Elert, Werner, *Abendmahl und Kirchengemeinschaft in der alten Kirche hauptsächlich des Ostens.* 1954. p. 42. Elert establishes his thesis with an allusion to Paul, who—with the exception of Ephesians and Colossians —"usually speaks of *ekklesia* only in connection with the name of a place—and accordingly speaks of the '*ekklesiai*' in the plural." Yet *ekklesia* in the singular appears in Paul in some decisive places; e.g., 1 Cor. 1: 2, 10: 32, 11: 22, 15: 9; Gal. 1-13; Phil. 3-6. For Paul, even the Corinthian "local congregation," sundered by party divisions, is an *ekklesia* of God in unity, in this sense, despite all the discord and coarse sinners with whom the members of the congregation should "also not eat" (1 Cor. 5:11). And also of the Galatian congregations, Paul speaks of a unit (Gal. 3:28). The ἐκκλησία τοῦ θεοῦ is alleged of all the several *ekklesiai* as the one people of God in its unity.

[2] Elert. *Ibid.*, p. 56.

[3] Elert, *Ibid.*, p. 42. A limitation must be made here in so far as the "polemical marks" are not so applicable against "schismatics" and "heretics" as against sinners in the congregations and against the rebellious "Israel."

Basic Considerations with Reference to Article VII of the Augsburg Confession

By Prof. Ernst Kinder

IN KEEPING WITH the scope of its content, Art. VII of the Augsburg Confession should really have the title "On the True Unity of the Church." It offers no thoughtful deductions on the nature of the church, but takes the reality of the church as given, and the short "definition" of the church which it offers (which is no creative definition), is only the presupposition for that which is said in the main part of the article on "the true unity of the church." This emphasis is to be understood from the situation behind the Augsburg Confession. The adherents of the Lutheran Reformation were charged by the papists with leaving the one historically-received Church of Jesus Christ in order to found a new, heretical church next to it. Against this charge, the Augsburg Confession wants to prove that its adherents have not deviated from the one, true Church of Jesus Christ; indeed, that they are more faithful to its *proprium* and more properly in keeping with the "true treasure" of the church, and thereby the church

[59]

itself, than are the papists. For the Lutherans confess the gospel to be the true center of the Church of Jesus Christ and judge and measure everything else in the church by it.

The Reformers could not conceive of the church other than as the *one* founded by Christ and preserved by Him throughout all ages until the end of the world. The notion of several confessional churches side by side would have been completely impossible for them. There is always only one Church of Jesus Christ which, to be sure, can be diabolically distorted into "no-church" or "anti-church." The question is: Who has better, more correctly, and more organically, confessed the one Church of Jesus Christ—the papists, who proceed from the hierarchy and canon law, or the sons of the Reformation, who proceed from the gospel as the decisive core of the church? The one church is constituted neither by the Roman Catholics nor by the followers of the Reformation, but is given to both by Christ. Nor can one construct it theologically, for one always finds a spiritual reality of life already there. Nor can it be destroyed, for in one form or another the one Church of Jesus Christ will be on earth until the end of time. The question is only—how can one recognize and judge where it is to be found historically, and how can one participate in its fellowship in certainty? It is to *this* question that Art. VII of the Augsburg Confession addresses itself. It says first that the one church will always be there, and that it precedes all of our efforts for unity. Then it says how one may properly recognize this one existing Church of Jesus Christ. Finally, it explains how this one church can and should be brought to expression in accord with the measure of its true "distinguishing marks" in "true unity," i.e., in true church fellowship.

1.

Also they teach that the one holy church is to continue forever. Art. VII begins with this fundamental assertion. This "is" is neither a desire nor a postulate, but a confident confession of what *is:* the *one* church *will* always be there, *perpetua mansura!* We do not bear this responsibility, but it is guaranteed by the promise of Christ, "The gates of hell shall not prevail against it" (Matt. 16:18). The conviction that the one Church of Jesus Christ will always be there is a conviction of faith grounded in the promise of Jesus Christ. One can only confess this if one does not attempt to understand the peculiar reality of the church from its historical manifestations, or the intensity of faith of its members, but rather from the institution of Jesus Christ himself. And one must not consider this "institution" only as an act in the past—as if Christ had only "started" the church and then left its further development, expansion, and preservation up to the Christians—but rather that Christ remains the present subject of its life and work.

This is the fundamental way in which the Augsburg Confession views the church. It refuses to describe the church primarily in terms of a sacral institution, a hierarchy, or a canon law. It stresses, in contrast, that the church is a communion of faith. *Est autem ecclesia congregatio sanctorum.* This does not mean that the Augsburg Confession advocates a "congregationalism" which dams up a congregational nature of the church within itself. Nor does the community of faith carry the being of the church within itself; rather, it *becomes* itself through the gospel by which Christ himself works in the Holy Spirit. Behind the *est autem ecclesia congregatio sanctorum* stands not a period, but a comma, which is followed by the decisive relative clause which defines the whole: *in qua evangelium.* It is the gospel which makes the church the church, and in and through the gospel comes Christ. Not the self-gathered, but the gospel-gathered and maintained community of faith is the church; a congregation is the *"grex"* gathered and maintained by the voice of the Good Shepherd. Luther says essentially the same in the Smalcald Articles (Sect. III, Art. 12): "For, thank God, today a child seven years old knows what the church is, namely, the holy believers and lambs who hear the voice of the Shepherd" (John 10:3). The voice of the Good Shepherd which makes and maintains the community of faith as a church belongs to the very heart of the definition of its nature.

When one views the church neither from its human administrations and arrangements (institutionally), nor from its members (sociologically), but fundamentally from its head Christ (Christologically), then one must say that the unity of the church is already there and that we always come from it. It is a fact established through Christ and guaranteed in Christ as the living Lord of the church. Our Lord's request in His high priestly prayer "that they might all be one" (John 17:21) is no longer simply a pious wish. It has truly been fulfilled in the completion of the sacrifice for which the Lord was preparing himself in this high priestly prayer (John 11:5ff.; Eph. 2:15ff). Since the reconciling sacrifice of Jesus Christ, His exaltation to the right hand of the Father, and the outpouring of the Holy Spirit, the unity of the new people of God is no longer wish and promise, but reality.

[61]

The first thing, then, which Art. VII has to say to us concerning the unity of the church is that it has long since been given, and that it will always be there. This is witnessed to by Eph. 4:4-6 on which Art. VII grounds its confession in the unity of the church: As truly as there is only *one* God, there is also only *one* people of God; as truly as there is only *one* Christ, there is only *one* body of Christ; and as truly as there is only *one* Holy Spirit, there is only *one* "called, gathered, enlightened, sanctified Christian Church kept in union with Jesus Christ," as Luther says in the explanation of the Third Article of the Apostles' Creed in the Small Catechism. The unity of the church, then, is not primarily a problem or a question, but a given fact; not a task, but a gift; not a goal to which we advance, but rather the presupposition and foundation from whence we come. It is the solid point from which we proceed. To be sure, many more serious things must be said about the unity of the church. But it would all be distorted and perverted if this given unity were not first asserted with unshakable certainty. And regarding that which must still be said concerning the unity of the church—the purpose of our efforts and endeavors is clearly not to effect, create, or make the church's unity. God does that himself in Christ and through the Holy Spirit. The church's unity, therefore, always precedes all of our efforts and endeavors. Only on the fixed basis of this certainty of faith will our efforts for the unity of the church receive their proper direction and perspective.

2.

We further assert that Art. VII of the Augsburg Confession speaks in a peculiar twofold manner in regard to the church: on the one hand, in demonstrative assertions of what *is,* and on the other hand, in hortative expressions of what *should be.* Basic, as said, is the first group which points in faithful confession to the givenness of the unity of the church from the Triune God. But now a "should" is set forth on the basis of this "is": "for the true unity of the church, it is enough that . . ." Here it becomes clear that the "being" of the church, which the faith given by the Triune God confesses, is not an "objective," reposing, secure "being," which is untempted and automatically self-manifesting *ex opere operato.* The realities of faith are such that even in their givenness they also include an appeal to those who confess them, so that the gift *(Gabe)* is also a responsibility *(Aufgabe)* for them. Hence, one cannot confess the unity of the church as a spectator from a subject-object distance, but only as one who permits himself to be held responsible for the unity given. We also find this doubleness of "what is" and "what should be" in Eph. 4: in verses 4-6, we hear testimony of the unity of the church as given by the Triune God; in verse 3, we hear the admonition to put this unity into practice: *"Endeavor to keep the unity!"*

We said that the confession of the already-existing unity of the church is an expression of faith. It is no "obvious" confession, but one which is made contrary to evidence. The unity of the church given by the Triune God is not an observable fact; it is a "hidden" reality. *Non est res tam vulgaris, Mi Erasme, Ecclesia Dei, quam est nomen hoc: Ecclesia Dei, . . . abscondita est ecclesia,* said Luther in *De servo Arbitrio.* The Apology of the Augsburg Confession (VII) puts it this way: *sub cruce tecta.* Yet the hidden unity of the church will not remain in the sphere of pure "invisibility." There is some Protestant talk about the invisibility of the church which reveals evaporation, irresponsibility, and flight. The unity of the church given by the Triune God can never become completely empirically visible, but remains hidden like its head (for non-believers) and like a side of its members (also for faith). (Here we could also speak at length of the human sins and the devilish powers of opposition in the church which can never overcome the church, but which can distort it tremendously.) And yet something of this hidden unity of the church always becomes empirically visible, taking on expression and effectiveness. Though the unity of the church cannot and should not become manifest through a *societas externarum rerum,* it nevertheless does not remain merely as a *civitas Platonica* (Apology VII).

This, however, places tasks and responsibilities upon the members of the church who confess in faith the unity of the church. Though it is not our responsibility to institute the unity of the church, it definitely is our responsibility to permit the unity of the church given in Christ and the Holy Ghost to make itself visible and efficacious in the right way at the right place. The unity of the church, as given by Christ and recognized and confessed by faith, should come to historical expression and power through the service and conduct of those who believe and confess in it. Those who really believe and confess the unity of the church also practice and witness to this unity with an inner power and holy zeal. Though they are not concerned with establishing the church's unity, they are concerned with its proper actualization.

3.

Since the unity of the church is already given by Christ, our efforts for its proper realization and actualization are provided thereby with their necessary norms and criteria. Hence Art. VII of the Augsburg Confession speaks of the *notae verae ecclesiae* (substantially, the expression itself is to be found in the Apology VII), which are at the same time the *regulae verae unitatis ecclesiae*. In our ecumenical efforts to bring about the realization of the hidden unity of the church, we cannot carry on arbitrarily as we please, in order to bring about unity at any cost, as long as it appears to us to be most pleasing, useful, impressive—or, according to the law of least resistance, the most easy way possible! Rather, our efforts are to be bound by the criteria which are given to us by Christ from the reality of the church itself. We should not aim at church unity with any methods or at any cost, but rather in keeping with its institution and continual maintenance by Christ.

What are these criteria by which we can judge whether or not an historical church unity is legitimate, i.e., in keeping with the hidden essential unity of the church? Fundamentally, we must say that those organs by which Christ in the Holy Ghost creates His one church as His body, preserving, erecting, ruling, and keeping it alive, also provide the criteria and standards for the proper actualization of the unity of the church in the world. This is to say that the legitimate, genuine actualization of the unity of the church must consist in its communal recognition and practice of those means of grace which were instituted by Christ and taken into service by the Holy Spirit. That which Christ instituted as necessary for the church's life and being must provide the unity principle for the legitimate realization and actualization of the true unity of the church. Which are these means of grace which Christ instituted as necessary for the church's life and which we hold to be normative for judging the true actualization of the unity of the church in life? With this question we confront the difficult crisis situation which now obtains in ecumenical circles where no existing standards are universally acknowledged, and where the *notae verae ecclesiae* are interpreted differently in the several churches.

The peculiar problem and emergency in the ecumenical movement today is not that there are various "churches." This situation can and must prevail without, in and of itself, doing violence to the unity of the church. The church's unity does not unconditionally need a centralized unity of organization as an expression of legal or administrative uniformity. Indeed, this would be neither good nor desirable, for then it could easily distort the uniqueness of the church and shift its central emphasis. On historical, political, and practical grounds, there can and may exist churches side by side with varying organizations, jurisdictions, administrations, and external forms. And we may call these "churches" on the authority of the New Testament, since the one church of Jesus Christ manifests itself characteristically in such historical *ecclesiae*. Nor would the existence, as such, of such different churches contradict the unity of the church *if* these different churches practiced church fellowship *(Kirchengemeinschaft)* with one another. It is our conviction that *church fellowship among historical churches* is the most fitting way in which to bring the integral unity of the church of Jesus Christ to expression and reality.

The peculiar crisis situation in ecumenical circles, therefore, consists not in the fact that there are different churches, but that there are divided churches, i.e., that the differences are partially *exclusive* which make church fellowship impossible between them. This means that some churches deny the character of the true church in other churches (i.e., that the one Church of Jesus Christ truly manifests itself there), addressing them as falsified churches and in heresy, and consequently breaking off church fellowship with them. Most of them do not do this out of a lesser ethos, such as obstinacy, caprice, or narrow-mindedness, but rather out of a sense of obedience and responsibility to their understanding of the true nature of the church. They cannot do otherwise without themselves betraying what they hold to be the true nature of the church. These exclusive differences and divisions which constitute the real ecumenical problem, however, are no longer to be explained as merely "harmless." There is something absurd, evil, and devilish at work here!

Some kind of limitation to church fellowship obtains for all churches, even for the most "free." No church is completely open; for each there comes a point beyond which it cannot go. Some draw the boundaries narrowly, others widely. All, however, draw the boundaries on different levels and in accordance with different standards. All vary in judging which standards are decisive, the accents upon importance and necessity depending upon the differing interpretations of the nature of the church. The dilemma of the ecumenical movement lies in the lack of agreement on criteria which could tell which differences are "harmless" and bearable—and thereby permitting the continuation of church fellowship—and which differences are so serious and unbearable that church fellowship is no longer possible. We lack the common standards for saying where we can be generous with others for the sake of fellowship, and where we must be stricter for the sake of truth. At variance also are the standards governing where we dare and dare not relativize in our quest both for church fellowship and obedient responsibility. Hence, we all view differently the possible ways for overcoming these divisions barring the way for church fellowship. Along with all the other member bodies of the World Council of Churches, even the "most conservative" wish to repudiate their exclusiveness, and even the "most free" recognize that there must be some binding criteria for church fellowship among them all. The ecumenical problem centers, then, on the need for universally recognized standards and guides for genuine church fellowship.

4.

We will now investigate what the evangelical position of the Lutheran Reformation is on this issue, and what positive contributions the Lutheran churches have to offer to this problem. The Lutheran Reformation was determined by its evangelical disposition to assert that only that may be established as necessary in and for the church which works by virtue of a clear divine mandate and clear divine promise for salvation. "For what is necessary [for the church] is that which makes good Christians; if it does not make good Christians, it is not [necessary for the church]." (Luther, *Vom Papstum zu Rom.* 1520, W. A. 6, 294). What is not creative and necessary for salvation dare not be declared as necessary for the church. Now it is *alone the gospel* of the saving and recreating grace of God in Jesus Christ which works human salvation; so also is the gospel alone peculiarly creative in the church. Through this gospel, the Holy Ghost creates, enlivens, builds, and sustains the church as the body of Christ. In the gospel, Christ himself is present, working, and ruling. *In verbo evangelii est ecclesia constructa* (W. A. 4, 189); *per evangelium aedificatur ecclesia constructa* (Ibid., p. 415). *Evangelium est sceptrum regale Christi in ecclesia sua* (W. A. 3, 32).

Therefore, the gospel alone must be declared to be unconditionally necessary for the church. That does not mean a mystical or dynamistic haziness and spiritualistic evaporation for the church. The gospel, by virtue of its own spiritually creative dynamic, has its own contours and norms. This is because it comes from the divine revelation of salvation witnessed to in Holy Scripture, and issues forth in the God-ordained concrete channels of the oral sermon and the sacrament in their salvatory and church-creating purpose. *Hence, the proclamation of the gospel according to the Biblical canon and the administration of the sacraments according to the institution of Christ* constitute the sole but also indispensable necessities in and for the church.

Art. VII of the Augsburg Confession asserts that where the gospel is "purely" proclaimed—i.e., according to the Biblical canon—and the sacraments are "rightly" administered—i.e., according to the institution of Christ—there is the Church of Jesus Christ at work. There God the Holy Ghost certainly creates and builds the one body around the one head, and calls and gathers men into this communal life and sanctifies them therein. "Word and sacrament" are not static distinguishing features, but rather working media of the Holy Ghost which have the promise that they will work faith and build the church. *Nam per verbum et sacramentum tamquam per instrumenta donatur spiritus sanctus, qui fidem efficit, ubi et quando visum est Deo, in his, qui audiunt evangelium* (Art. V). Because of this, the hidden Church of Jesus Christ is to be recognized in history by "Word and sacrament."

"One can truly recognize the Christian congregation where the pure gospel is preached. Just as a military banner provides us with a certain sign by which to identify its lord and army, so too by the gospel one can tell where Christ and His army lie as is promised to us in Isaiah 55:11." (Luther, W. A. 11, 408). "Baptism, Holy Communion and the gospel are the external signs whereby we can tell where the church is in the world . . . For where baptism, Holy Communion and the gospel are, no one should doubt that there are saints there who are at the same time merely children in the cradle" (W. A. 6, 301. *Ecclesia non est tantum societas externarum rerum ac rituum . . . , sed principaliter est societas fidei et spiritus sancti in cordibus, qua tamen habet externas notas, ut agnosci possit, videlicet puram evangelii doctrinam* (i.e., proclamation) *et administrationem sacramentorum consentaneam evangelio Christi. Et haec ecclesia sola dicitur corpus Christi, quod Christus spiritu sancto renovat, sanctificat et gubernat* (Apology, VII, 5).

And as the Church of Jesus Christ is to be recognized historically in "Word and sacrament," so, too, "Word and sacrament" provide the criteria whereby we may judge where that true church fellowship takes place which manifests the unity of the church which is given through Christ. Where, in different "churches," the one same gospel is purely proclaimed and the sacraments rightly administered, there the one same Church of Jesus Christ is present and at work, however else they may appear to be different from each other on the surface. Where unity is given as a gift in the center and heart of the church, there the gift of true church fellowship is also given by Christ himself through His instituted means of work. The viewpoint of the Lutheran Reformation does not judge and measure the matter of church fellowship from the boundaries of the church— as by considering the quality of its members or its organization—but rather from the center of its operation which has a clear divine mandate and promise for the church. Christ himself, working creatively in the church, grants true church fellowship wherever this principle is clearly recognized and practiced. *True church fellowship, then, consists essentially in proclamation and sacramental fellowship.*

It is not enough, however, that the pure proclamation of the gospel and the proper administration of the sacraments are merely *somehow* present or practiced in the various churches. Somehow—if only in part—they are present in all churches. Hence, partial church fellowship obtains more or less among them all. A complete, inclusive church fellowship, on the other hand, can only be present where there is also a mutually recognized and acknowledged *consensus de doctrina evangelii et de administratione sacramentorum.* Pure proclamation of the gospel and proper administration of the sacrament are not only *somehow* to be in the church; they are to be consciously known and recognized as such. For "Word and sacrament" do not work automatically in and for the church, but only through human responsibility. There is a normative quality to "pure" and "proper." Therefore the church cannot tolerate hovering indifference, but it calls for decision and public affirmation. The binding of the proclamation to Holy Scripture and the binding of the administration to its institution are not merely to be affirmed in general or postulated in principle by the church. They must rather be bound together organically with all names named. For, as said, the gospel is not only a certain actual dynamic; its content is also filled with the salvatory revelation of God, finding its norm in the original Biblical testimony. Therefore its decisive central point and profile necessitates that it be taken up responsibly by the church with all names named. The church, then, cannot draw back to a pure objectivism in regard to the gospel and the "means of grace"; the gospel which it carries and by which it is carried always calls it to confessing decisions of truth.

The confession of the church is the answer of the community of the faithful to the gospel which has founded it and with which it has been entrusted. The church as church stands or falls in so far as it is true in its witness to the decisive content of the gospel. This confessing answer by the community of faith is itself elicited by the gospel. The confession of the church is an expression of obedience to the gospel. Without such a confessing acceptance and acknowledgment, the gospel—as the *Word* of God—will not go forth fruitfully in and for the church. In his work, *Von den Conziliis und von der Kirche*, 1539, Luther asserts the Word of God as the distinguishing mark of the true church: "We speak here of the external Word, orally preached through men like you and me, for such is what Christ left behind [instituted] as an external sign by which one could recognize His Church or His holy people. We speak also of such oral Word so that it may be earnestly believed and publicly confessed before the world, as Christ says, 'Whosoever therefore shall confess me before men, him will I also confess before my Father and his angels' (Matt. 10:32; Luke 12:8). For there are many who know secretly who will not confess it publicly . . ." And Luther can also say, *Propter confessionem coetus ecclesiae est visibilis . . . Ex confessione cognoscitur ecclesia* (W. A. 39, II, 161).

This does not mean that the confession constitutes the church and creates church fellowship. Christ alone does that through the gospel in Word and sacrament. In this constitutive sense, Word and sacrament alone are the *notae ecclesiae*. In this sense, the confession of the church is not one of the *notae ecclesiae*. But as the conscious acceptance and acknowledgment of that which does constitute the church and as the common self-relating of the church to its unique *notae*, the confession remains the *conditio sine qua non* for the fruitful course of the gospel through Word and sacrament. Therefore, without such a common confession of the gospel and without such a declared fidelity of the church to it, no genuine church fellowship can exist which is not also *confessional fellowship*. While it is not grounded in a common confession, church fellowship will also demonstrate itself in this manner. Hence, Art. VII of the Augsburg Confession states, *Ad veram unitatem ecclesiae satis est consentire de doctrina evangelii et de administratione sacramentorum*. So there will be a desire to express and demonstrate in a declaration of common consensus that church fellowship, as proclamation and sacramental fellowship, really exists. Confessing agreement must be reached regarding what the central and decisive points of proclamation really are, what the proclamation of the gospel in keeping with Holy Scripture really is, and what the administration of the sacrament in keeping with its institution really is, if the church fellowship is to be genuine. This does not mean that uniformity must be reached on every single theological issue. We dare not confuse confession with theology, dogma with dogmatics. We are concerned here only with the central and the decisive, with those points of the salvatory revelation of God which are absolutely necessary for the life of the church. These the confession calls by name. And they are not, as outsiders often think, so difficult and complicated; in truth they are great and simple. In these, however, true unity must actually reign. Out of the decision of faith, the church in its confession lifts out the central and indispensable points of God's saving revelation as they are communally acknowledged as the binding guides for the proclamation of the gospel and the administration of the sacraments. Herein there must be unanimity if true church fellowship—as proclamation and sacramental fellowship—is to be practiced in a promising way.

The church fellowship given by Christ through Word and sacrament which is evidenced in common confession must also make clear where we believe the *boundaries* lie for promising church fellowship. These come to expression in the antitheses of the Confessions. Central to the confession is a common Yes to the basic and decisive points of the revelation of salvation as guidance for the proclamation of the Word and the administration of the sacraments. But for the sake of this public witness, the church must then also issue its No where the gospel demands it. The denials and rejections in the Confessions desire to be taken neither as moral defamation nor as a blanket refusal to recognize any of the true church in those against whom they are directed. They are never directed against a whole church as such, but only against definite, clearly named teachings which are opposed to the gospel, and therefore dangerous for salvation and destructive of church life. These antitheses assert that for the sake of the truth and credibility of the gospel, neither church fellowship nor proclamation and sacramental fellowship can be shared with those who hold and represent unacceptable doctrinal views. Just as the confession cannot constitute church fellowship, but rather confirms and acknowledges that which is already given by Christ through the gospel, so it cannot set any boundaries, but rather confirms and acknowledges those boundaries which are drawn already by Christ through the positive and negative assertions it has taken over from the Confessions of the early church and the Reformation, testing them continually against the gospel of Holy Scripture for verification. If the church is convinced that in these Confessions are to be found the "center and summary" of Holy Scripture and the "true treasure of the church" upon which the church as the Church of Jesus Christ must either stand or fall, then it cannot go contrary to the saving truth, but must acknowledge it even at the expense of church fellowship.

5.

Centrally important is the great *satis est* of Art. VII of the Augsburg Confession and all that is implied in it. Confessional agreement on the central and decisive points of the revelation of salvation is at once indispensable and all-sufficient for a promising church fellowship. When this agreement is given, so is church fellowship, and it should be joyfully and confidently acknowledged and practiced without any anxiety or qualms, for we may trust the decisive in the life of the church to the commonly-confessed gospel! And above and beyond this there dare not be demanded any more as a condition for the acknowledging and practicing of church fellowship. Everything else which is demanded as unconditionally necessary for the church and its fellowship with other churches are merely legalistic *notae* substituted for the true *notae* established by the gospel in and for the church. But the law does not quicken; it kills. It does not promote the true unity of the church in history; it hinders it. Hence, Art. VII declares, "*And to the true unity of the church . . . it is not necessary that human traditions, that is, rites or ceremonies, instituted by men, should be everywhere alike.*" These things must also be in the church, and in their place they can be very useful and helpful. But one dare not legislate these matters for fundamental freedom must rule here.

The allocation of importance and accentuation in Art. VII is of fundamental significance for the church and cannot be surrendered if the gospel is truly to rule in the church and to provide the standards for church fellowship. It must be stoutly maintained that only the standards derived from the gospel dare be considered as unconditionally necessary for the actualization and fellowship of the churches. Everything else must remain essentially in freedom. As strongly as the Lutheran church must insist upon confessional agreement on the centrality of the absolute gospel, just as decisively must it reject any legalistic attempts to establish criteria and conditions for church fellowship at any other places than the gospel. In our efforts to bring the unity of the church into expression as church fellowship, we dare not lay the accent on criteria for things which have no clear mandate or certain promise of the Lord for His Church.

Enough for the "true unity of the church"— church fellowship — is unity in regard to the living center and life-creating heart of the church, to Christ's means of grace and the Holy Ghost. Forms of church constitution and administration, liturgical orders, and the piety and way of life of the congregation, theological patterns and programs on the responsibility of the church for the world—all these have their importance and necessity in their place in the church, but none of these should have normative significance regarding either church division or church fellowship. Rather, these matters must be left free in the church, so that church fellowship may remain as long as agreement exists on the central matters, even where differences obtain in these other issues.

This does not say that more uniformity should not be attempted in these matters for the sake of love and peace and more effective service where it appears to be commanded without involving any compromise of conscience. One should be just as careful not to make a law out of the opposition to these things. We dare not distort Art. VII to read— as it often almost appears to sound in parts of Protestantism: "It is necessary for the true unity of the church that in all forms everything be as chaotic, unrestrained, and capricious as possible!" But even then we cannot give any unmediated saving value to these forms, and uniformity in them dare never be demanded.

The Lutheran Church can make a helpful contribution and offer an important service to our contemporary ecumenical efforts if it will remain true to the fundamental emphases and accentuations of Art. VII of the Augsburg Confession. To be sure, the precondition is that this perspective first be implemented among all the confessionally-bound Lutheran churches themselves. The Lutheran Church can take on its ecumenical responsibility and task in sharing what has especially been entrusted to it from the Reformation only after it has itself fulfilled the "Thou shalt" inherent in its gifts. The contemporary Lutheran churches must allow themselves to be asked by the Reformation, both individually and collectively, whether they are really true to the emphasis of Art. VII on the centrality of Christ and the *notae ecclesiae* given through the gospel. We must not treat these *notae* in a formalistic and legalistic fashion. Rather we must permit their essential content to take the central position in their own illuminating and convincing manner, and to allow all else really to be ruled by them. One must note that all this is not motivated by pedantic obstinacy, or because of jealous and fearful protection of one's confessional prestige, or for the sake of mere traditionalism and the like.

Instead, it is because of our concern for the Gospel of God as the true treasure of the *one* whole church. Nor dare this obtain only theoretically *de jure;* it must rather also be implemented *de facto* in practice.

From the basic perspective of the Reformation, then, the Lutheran churches bear an important and promising responsibility in the current ecumenical discussions on the proper manifestations of the unity of the church. They must witness and insist that the most promising way to unity is the way to the center. The more the Christian churches toil for unity in regard to the center established by Christ, all the more will the ecumenical efforts benefit from healthy profit and standards. In honorable and fraternal conversations with the other churches on the basis of the Holy Scripture, and with the full contribution of the Confessions, the Lutheran churches must work to win assent for the approach which sees the decisive center of the church in the salvation-creating gospel in Word and sacrament. This approach stresses the primary necessity of working for an inner agreement on central matters, rather than remaining with peripheral matters. Much has already been won for the true unity of the church if fundamental agreement has been achieved on which points one must be narrow, and on which one may be liberal.

Once this fundamental value scale is set, then one may work with others toward essential agreement on those issues which have been mutually accepted as central. To the extent to which this earnestly occurs, the Lutheran Church can and should be generous and liberal in regard to other secondary matters, and not be afraid to learn here from others. The Reformation concept of the church does not contain a complete blueprint for concrete construction of the church. It cites only the indispensable points, and is more a "compass" and value scale than a self-sufficient "Magna Charta" for the practical arrangements of the life of the church. Here we can and may take over much from others. Our teaching points us clearly enough to those elements in which we should work for the manifestation of the hidden unity of the church. The complete revelation of the hidden unity of the church will only be effected by the returning Lord himself. We should not postpone our efforts until then, however, but seriously devote ourselves now to those areas where our responsibility calls us to work while it is still day!

[73]

Church Unity and Sacramental Fellowship

By Bishop Anders Nygren

1. *The Church of Christ Is Only One*

EVERY ECUMENICAL CONSIDERATION of the question of the relation of the "churches" to each other must begin with the fact that by its very nature, the Church of Christ is one. Only because the unity of the church is already from the outset a *given* fact—independent of all that we do—does it have any meaning for us to strive for the unity of the church. The unity for which we strive can only mean that an already existing unity marks the life of the church communities ("churches") which should be expressed in external, tangible form.

From this point of departure in the unity of the church which already exists, all presumptions are rejected which would suggest that *we* could bring the church's unity into realization. We do not decree over the church, and cannot make anything out of it except that which it already is. The starting point for the ecumenical quest of unity is not the different "churches," and the goal dare not be the overcoming of the existing divisions in order to establish a "super-church" which

[75]

embraces all the different "churches" within itself. Such an undertaking would merely be man's work. But the church is not man's work; it is God's work, the work of the Holy Ghost. It is the Holy Ghost who "calls, gathers, enlightens, and sanctifies the whole Christian church on earth, and preserves it in union with Jesus Christ in the one true faith." Were the unity of the church only a future goal for the realization of which we had to work—and not a reality already given from God—then all of our work for unity would be doomed to failure from the very outset.

2. *The Unity of the Church Has Its Ground in Jesus Christ*

a) *The church as the body of Christ.* God has given Christ to the *ekklesia* as its head, and the *ekklesia* is the "body of Christ" (ἡ ἐκκλησία ἐστιν τὸ σῶμα ἀυτοῦ, Eph. 1:22ff.). Just as Adam is the head of the old humanity, and as humanity "in him"— its head — is placed under the power of sin and death, so too has God given mankind a new beginning through Christ. "In Christ" as the head of the new humanity, the head of the church, and the head of the new creation, we are placed under the power of righteousness and life. "For as in Adam (ἐν τῷ Ἀδὰμ) all die, even so in Christ (ἐν τῷ Χριστῷ) shall all be made alive" (1 Cor. 15:22). "Wherefore, as by one man sin entered into the world, and death by sin . . . For if by one man's offence death reigned by one; . . . they which receive the gift of righteousness shall reign in life by one, Jesus Christ" (Rom. 5:12ff.).

b) *The one and the many.* The grouping of the *one* and the *many* which we find in Romans 5 deserves special consideration, for it says something fundamental both about the Messianic mission of Jesus, and also about the relation of Christ to the church. Behind this lies the "suffering servant" conception of Isaiah 53: the *one* who sacrificed himself for *many*. The Messianic act of Christ consists in the fact that He, the *one* righteous person, took upon himself the destiny of the *many* sinners. "Surely he hath borne our griefs, and carried our sorrows; . . . The Lord hath laid upon him the iniquity of us all." "My righteous servant shall justify many, for he shall bear their iniquities." Employing these words of Isaiah 53 and the words of the "lamb who will be led to slaughter," John the Baptist says, "Behold the Lamb of God, which taketh away the sin of the world" (John 1:29). And using the word of "the many" from Isaiah 53, Jesus speaks at the institution of Holy Communion of "blood of the new testament, which is shed for many for the remission of sins" (Matt. 26:28; Mark 14:24).

The *one* for the *many*, the *righteous one* for the sinners. The gospel is not a narration of how it once went with *one* righteous man in this world, and how He lived His righteous life for His own sake. That would not be a proclamation of Christ the Messiah. Rather the content of the gospel is that the *one* was given for the *many*, the *righteous one* for the *sinners*. The one and the many are just that inseparable. The content of the gospel is the *unity* between the one and the many: "For he hath made him to be sin for us, who knew no sin; that we might be made the righteousness of God in him" (ἐν αὐτῷ, 2 Cor. 5: 21).

Here lies the ground of unity between Christ and the church. The self-sacrifice of Christ has its goal precisely in the church: "Christ loved the church and gave himself for it" (Eph. 5: 25), and the church has its ground absolutely in this self-sacrifice of Christ. Its whole being is a being ἐν Χριστῷ. If one can say that Christ is never without His Church, so it can also be said that the church is nothing without Christ. One cannot speak of the church without speaking of Christ. For the church without Christ is *nothing*. The church does not have its own being independent of Christ. The church is that for which Christ has given himself, and the church lives its life ἐν Χριστῷ. The word in Ephesians describing the church as "the body of Christ" is the deepest thing that can be said of it. It speaks of the indissoluble unity of the Church with Christ.

c) *Christ—the ground for the unity of the church.* With what has already been said we have also given the ground for the unity of the church. Just as Christ is *one*, so there can be only *one* body, only one σῶμα Χριστοῦ, only *one* Church of Christ. This unity of the church is essential. The goal of Christ's self-sacrifice was to make righteous men out of sinners, to make *one* out of many, "that one man Jesus should die . . . in order that he might gather together in one the children of God that were scattered abroad" (συναγάγῃ εἰς ἕν. John 11: 50ff). According to Paul, life in Christ, i.e., being members of the body of Christ, means that *one* will result from the many: For we, the *many*, are one body in Christ" (οὕτως οἱ πολλοὶ ἕν σῶμά ἐσμεν ἐν Χριστῷ, Rom. 12: 5).

What the unity of the church means can best be seen in Eph. 4: 4ff.: "There is one body, and one Spirit, even as ye are called in one hope of your calling; one Lord, one faith, one baptism, one God and Father of all, who is above all, and through all, and in you all." These words contain a mighty confession on the unity of the church; it is set in parallel with the unity of God. Just as there is *one* God who does not tolerate other gods at his side (First Commandment.), and as there is only *one* Lord and Savior (Acts 4:12; Heb. 7:27; Phil. 2:9; Matt. 28:18), so there is only *one* church, only *one* body of Christ. To eliminate the unity of the church is to eliminate the church itself.

Therefore the division within the church is such a serious matter. God joined together the body of Christ out of its different members, "so that there should be no more schism in the body" (1 Cor. 12:24ff.). To break the unity of the church is an attack upon the body of Christ, and consequently, upon Christ himself. "Is Christ divided?" (1 Cor. 1:13).

3. *The Unity of the Church in Art. VII of the Augsburg Confession*

It is striking that Art. VII of the *Confessio Augustana*—the section which is rightly regarded as the *locus classicus* in the Lutheran Confessions "on the church"— takes as its peculiar theme just this question of the *unity* of the church. Of all the questions which could be treated in connection with the church, the problem of its unity is placed in the center of the foreground. (a) The Article begins with the confession, *quod una sancta ecclesia perpetuo mansura sit.* (b) It then states wherein "the true unity of the church" is to be found. (c) After this it formulates what "is not necessary" for the unity of the church. (d) Finally, it concludes with the great confession of the church in Eph. 4:5ff.: "One body, one Spirit, one hope, one Lord, one faith, one baptism, one God and Father of all." Clearly, unity is here the chief consideration.

a) It has sometimes been alleged that the designation *Una sancta* was something specially characteristic of the Roman Catholic understanding of the church. Art. VII of the Augsburg Confession convinces us of the opposite. It freely employs the expression *Una sancta* as a designation of the church, though in a totally different sense from the one common in the imperialistic Roman usage. It speaks of the *unity* of the church in its New Testament meaning. Even if the Roman Church used this same word to give expression to its claim to be the only true church, still the Lutheran Confessions refuse to surrender the New Testament understanding of the term as an expression for the fact that the Church of Christ is *one.* Faith in the *Una sancta* is anchored in the gospel itself, and it is inseparable from faith in Christ and in the Holy Ghost. Just as Christ is with us every day until the end of the world, so also will His Church stand— *perpetuo mansura*—throughout all the change of time: "the gates of hell shall not prevail against it." (Matt. 16:18).

Where is the *one* Church of Christ? An old answer has it that the church is there where the bishop is (Cyprian). On this foundation the Roman Church has built further. The Reformation demands that we dig deeper. Its answer is essentially this: *the church is where Christ is.* Where Christ is, there by necessity is also σῶμα Χριστοῦ. Where Christ is, there is also the people of God whom He has come to lead together into *oneness.*

The church is where Christ is. And where is Christ? He is present *in his Word and in the sacraments.* Life "in Christ" comes about through the Word, through the Word of the gospel: "Ye abide in me and my words abide in you" (John 15:7). "The gospel of Christ . . . is the power of God unto salvation to everyone that believeth" (Rom. 1:16). Where the Gospel of Christ is proclaimed, there is not merely narrated something which once happened, but there Christ himself is present with His *dynamis* and frees us from the power of the forces of evil and places us within the life "in Christ." The same is true of the sacraments. In *baptism,* we are engrafted "in Christ," the true vine. On the basis of our baptism we are no longer to live only for ourselves (Gal. 2:20). Through baptism we are made members of the body of Christ and "have been planted together" (σύμφυτοι) to share in His death and resurrection (Rom 6:5). Through baptism we have departed from the body of sin and death (τὸ σῶμα τῆς ἁμαρτίας, Rom. 6:6; τὸ σῶμα τοῦ θανάτου Rom. 7:24), and are transplanted into the body of Christ, "in Christ," who is our righteousness and life. *Holy Communion* is ultimately "the communion of the body of Christ" (1 Cor. 10:16). In Holy Communion, Christ himself is present with His *dynamis* and makes us partakers of His body. "Take, eat, this is my body" (1 Cor. 11:24).

In this powerful presence of Christ in His dealings with us through Word and sacrament, it is firmly established that we can speak only of the one Church of Christ. Where Christ is, there is the church. There all who believe are gathered together into a *unity* in Christ.

Art. VII of the Augsburg Confession summarizes this all as follows: "The church is the congregation of saints in which the gospel is rightly taught and the sacraments are rightly administered" (*est autem ecclesia congregatio sanctorum, in qua evangelium recte docetur et recte sacramenta administrantur*).

Where the gospel and the sacraments are operative in accord with Christ's commission and direction, there is Christ himself in action with His effective promise of the forgiveness of sins and with His incorporation of men into the body of Christ. Where this activity takes place, there is *most certainly* the church.

Since we have employed the traditional formula, "the Word and the sacraments," it is to be noted that the expression "the Word" is used here in the same sense as "the gospel." Regarding this passage in Art. VII, Prof. E. Schlink has properly noted, "We must take notice of the fact that it is neither the Word of God in general nor the law which is here named, but solely the gospel, and that in connection with 'preaching'" (*Theologie der Lutherischen Bekenntnisschriften,* 2d Ed., p. 269.) This indicates where the main point lies, and that it is the real presence of Christ in the gospel and the sacraments which is treated throughout. The gospel is God's Word filled with power (δύναμις θεοῦ), i.e., God's mighty deed for the redemption of man (Rom. 1:16). For through the gospel God's righteousness is proclaimed and God's righteousness is given (Rom. 1:17).

b) Wherein, then, lies *the true unity of the church?* The answer has already been given. Where the gospel and sacraments are operative, there is Christ, and He is himself the unity of the church. That is, *Ad veram unitatem ecclesiae satis est consentire de doctrina evangelii et administratione sacramentorum.* Two further comments deserve mention here.

1) That the gospel and sacraments are necessary and indispensable presuppositions both for the existence and the unity of the church is unquestionably clear. Where the gospel of Christ is not proclaimed, and the incorporation in Christ through the sacraments does not take place, there Christ is not present, and consequently there is no church. The Augsburg Confession, therefore, could have said, *Ad veram unitatem ecclesiae necesse est.* . . . Instead of this, it actually reads, *Ad veram unitatem ecclesiae satis est.* . . . In this context, both formulations mean the same thing. Yet it is interesting to note that the latter formulation has an entirely different *ecumenical* ring to it. One can presume that every Christian Church would be true to the gospel and administer the sacraments in accordance with the instruction of the Lord. And when this is the case, one can say, "satis est." "It is enough for the true unity of the Christian Church to agree concerning the doctrine of the gospel and the administration of the sacraments." With this *satis est,* one is already halfway to the next sentence with its *nec necesse est:* "Nor is it necessary to the true unity of the Christian Church." It is *enough* with this—nothing else is necessary: both of these express one and the same thought. The gospel and the sacraments are necessary for the unity of the church, but they are also the *only* necessities.

2) What is meant by *consentire de doctrina evangelii?* The German text renders this roughly as follows, "that the gospel be preached

harmoniously and with pure understanding." The word *doctrina* here does not have the unavoidably intellectualistic meaning which it has come to have for us. *Docere* and "preaching" are interchangeable here. What is required is that the gospel be preached in keeping with its own meaning, that the message which God sent out in the gospel should be carried on and received in exactly the same meaning by us. The norm for that which should be preached is not a fixed *doctrina* in addition to the gospel, but it is rather the gospel itself, "the gospel according to pure understanding." We arrive at the same conclusion if we address our attention to the concept *consentire*. For the *consensus* which is meant here is not founded upon confessional formulae to which all have bound themselves, but rather "that the gospel be preached harmoniously and with pure understanding." Nothing at all is said here about a confession; only the gospel is being discussed. It has to do with the gospel in operation, and there no confessional formulae can produce a conclusive guarantee. Only in the willingness to humble oneself under the gospel, in giving up all one's own contrary thoughts and interpretations, and in allowing oneself to be taught by the gospel, can this *consensus* be created. Christ is the head of the church; the Gospel of Christ is its only norm. Where the church of Christ is, there is the subordination to the gospel. And again: where this subordination under the gospel is to be found, there is the church of Christ.

c) Once it has been established that it is enough for the unity of the church that the gospel be purely preached and the sacraments rightly administered, then it is already said that *nothing* else is necessary for the unity of the church. Often it has been demanded as necessary for the unity of the church that a process of uniformity take place in the various "churches" in order for all to assume the same church orders, the same confessional formulae, the same rites and ceremonies. Now it is not to be opposed if a greater unanimity be carried out in various parts of the church—but this must occur in freedom. Freedom reigns in the church, and freedom should reign. Where the one necessity of dependence upon Christ and His Gospel is observed, there should be freedom in all other things. There is room for historical multiplicity. The unity of the church cannot disturb this. In short, *Nec necesse est ubique esse similes traditiones humanas, seu ritus aut ceremonias ab hominibus institutas.*

This means, however, at the same time, that any attempt to make a necessary presupposition for the unity of the church out of something which the gospel leaves free, is a distortion of the gospel itself.

Such means only establish disorder and division in the Church of Christ.

4. *Consequences for Ecclesiastical and Sacramental Fellowship*

Since the Church of Christ is *one,* it follows of necessity that there be ecclesiastical and sacramental fellowship *(Kirchen- und Abendmmahlsgemeinschaft)* among the various parts of the one church. When two "churches" each preach the gospel purely and administer the sacraments in accord with the instructions of the Lord, but for some other reason have broken off fellowship with one another, there still remains between them the deeper community "in Christ." They are counted as members of the same body of Christ, and this community cannot be abrogated merely by external resolutions. The same holds true for sacramental fellowship. It is extant wherever the Church of Christ is. Even where two church communions refuse "sacramental fellowship" with each other, and maintain that they cannot meet each other at the Lord's Table, they cannot break the community which is already grounded in the fact that they both—each for himself—are partaking of the one bread. "For we being many are one bread, and one body; for we are all partakers of that one bread" (1 Cor. 10:17).

From this perspective, the guiding principles are clear for the fellowship of the "churches" with one another. It is also clear how serious a question ecclesiastical and sacramental fellowship really is. We may formulate two fundamental principles: 1) Where the deeper unity "in Christ" exists between two "churches," it must also manifest itself in some form of ecclesiastical and sacramental fellowship. 2) Where the deeper unity "in Christ" is lacking, it dare not be feigned by external ecclesiastical and sacramental fellowship.

There are well-known instances where a "church" has so completely fallen away from the Gospel of Christ that it dare not be considered any longer as a member of the body of Christ. No ecclesiastical fellowship dare be maintained with such a pseudo-church. It is presupposed in this case that the apostasy from the gospel is already a definitive and conclusive fact. The Galatian congregations had allowed themselves to be "removed unto another gospel" (Gal. 1:6). Nevertheless, Paul writes to them as the *ekklesiai* in Galatia. He does not break off fellowship because "there are some that trouble you and would pervert the gospel of Christ" (Gal. 1:7). He speaks his anathema, his *damnamus,* over the false proclamation, but he holds fast to the fellowship with the "brothers" (Gal. 1:9,11) since they were misled and could be corrected.

To abrogate church fellowship is a very serious matter, for it means fundamentally that the excluded "church" is not considered a real church. For if it is a member of the body of Christ, then fellowship actually exists with the whole σῶμα Χριστοῦ. To deny this church fellowship is the same as "dividing" Christ (1 Cor. 1:13).

The normal relation between Christian "churches" should be church fellowship. They should recognize each other as members of the same body of Christ without previous agreements and proclamations. Excluding a "church" from church fellowship is the abnormal case, and this must be done by other "churches" only "with fear and trembling" in remembrance of Rom. 14:4, "Who art thou that judgest another man's servant? To his own master he standeth or falleth." Or again in 1 Cor. 10:12, "Wherefore let him that thinketh that he standeth take heed lest he fall." In all this, the gospel alone must be the standard, and not any human traditions, orders, or habits of thought.

How should this ecclesiastical fellowship, this communion between the "churches"— or better said — this fellowship within the Church of Christ, concretely take on form? And what kind of sacramental fellowship should be striven for? In the ecumenical discussions, ecclesiastical and sacramental fellowship has been graduated according to varying grades. So, for example, the mutual "celebration" of the sacrament by ministers of different "churches" (confessions) is considered a more perfect community than where "only" the members of the different "churches" are mutually admitted as communicants.

To see clearly here, we must relate the question to the basic principles spelled out above. For if one leaves the deeper unity already given "in Christ" out of consideration, then one seeks to recapture the lost unity by constantly raising the demands for external community with total uniformity and organizational unity as the goal.

Who has said that the ecclesiastical and sacramental community which exists among the members of the body of Christ (because of the unity of the church with Christ) should make itself known in "inter-celebration"? Holy Communion has its place in the life of the local congregation. It is not celebrated in general, but rather in a concrete congregation, here and now. There Christ is with His Church and in His Church. Here, in this local congregation, the one Church of Christ makes its appearance. And it does not in the slightest become more of the Church of Christ merely because the ministers of different "churches" participate. The unity of the church is given in the presence of Christ, and this unity becomes neither smaller nor greater through the presence and assistance of ministers from various "churches." The unity of the church is belied, and Christ is "divided," however, when the reception of the sacrament is limited in principle to only the members of each "church," and when members of other "churches" are thereby excluded in principle.

The grounds for the ecclesiastical and sacramental fellowship which must prevail in the Church of Christ are as follows:

(1) That the "churches" mutually acknowledge each other as members of the body of Christ.

(2) That they acknowledge the validity of Holy Communion in other "churches" when it is carried out in accord with the institution of Christ.

(3) That they admit members of other "churches" to the Lord's Table in their own congregations.

Where these three practices prevail, the unity of the Church of Christ is brought to expression in the concrete life of the local congregation.

Now what are the difficulties which obstruct the way for such ecclesiastical and sacramental fellowship as understood above? In the various traditions, the difficulties arise at different points. I will cite here only four examples.

(1) For most "churches," there is a common foundation in the recognition of each other's baptism as the incorporation of one "in Christ" and in His Church. Here the Baptist interpretation provides considerable difficulty. This is also recognized by them. A Baptist author writes, "It should be admitted without reservation that the heaviest stumbling block for Christian fellowship beyond the boundaries of the several communities lies precisely in our interpretation of baptism." This interpretation appears to mean a fundamental judgment passed upon all other "churches." Often, however, this consequence is not drawn. The quoted author writes of the other "churches," "We openly and willingly recognize them as *branches of the Church of Christ.* But the congregational ideal which they represent is not in accord with our understanding of the New Testament."

(2) The difficulty which ecclesiastical and sacramental fellowship faces from the *Orthodox* and *Anglican* side is connected with the doctrine of ordination and the *successio apostolica.* Even if the Anglican Church does not recognize ordination as a sacrament, it is still set up by many as a necessary presupposition for the "validity" of Holy Communion and for complete ecclesiastical fellowship with other "churches." Along with the presence of Christ in the gospel and the sacraments, the notion of church "order" is also introduced. It must

meanwhile be remembered, however, that the Anglican side in general does not deny that non-episcopal "churches" are members of the body of Christ. Not even the Orthodox Church has exhibited a complete unanimity in rejection of non-episcopal "churches" (cf. the discussion between Archbishop Germanos and Prof. Arseniev in Edinburgh in the official (German) Conference Report, 1940, p. 290).

(3) Still another difficulty presents itself in the interpretation of the *Society of Friends,* where both the sacraments and the "outer Word" are placed secondary to the "inner Light." In so far as this "inner Light" is meant to express the same as "Christ in us," however, it appears that a certain agreement with the "churches" is possible.

(4) From the Lutheran side, subscription to the Lutheran confession has sometimes been viewed as a presupposition for ecclesiastical and sacramental community. Here it must be pointed out again that in Art. VII of the Augsburg Confession, the *satis est* refers only to the gospel and the sacraments. Where these are actually in operation, everything necessary is present for the unity of the church.

The more that Christ—as present in His church in Word and sacrament—is permitted to stand in the central position, and everything else that is important to us (be it a congregational ideal or church order or a dogmatic formulation) be valued as service to His presence, all the more will the unity of the church permeate.

If the various "churches" do maintain church fellowship despite disagreement on important teachings, it dare not lead to relativizing the content of the gospel. What is decisive is that the gospel be purely preached. Here the "churches" should help one another to drive always deeper into the gospel. Often that cannot take place except through serious struggle. But there will be struggles carried on *within* the church. Abrogation of church fellowship is no appropriate means. If a part of the church strays from the truth of the gospel, it must be restored again. Here we owe one another ruthless sincerity. There always have been and always will be serious disagreements within the church in order that the gospel, the true treasure of the church, may not be lost. If we maintain church fellowship to the utmost, then we must also engage in these disagreements within the community in all seriousness. These disagreements are always there, however, not in order that we may judge one another, but rather that we may help one another as far as possible in our common struggle for the whole truth. Then the struggle *within* the church will serve as the means whereby Christ builds up His body and strengthens its unity.

[85]

II

The Confession

The Present Significance of the Lutheran Confession

By Prof. Peter Brunner

THE LUTHERAN CONFESSION binds the congregations, its shepherds, and its teachers, exclusively to the apostolic gospel. The Lutheran confession, consequently, contains no self-reposing or self-subsistent truths All that is expressive of valid knowledge derives its validity from the apostolic gospel alone. It belongs to the inalienable foundaton of Luther's Reformation that the church cannot derive or establish any article of faith from itself. According to the Lutheran confession, what is not set forth as the content of faith through God's revelation in the Word of God can never become the content of any church dogma. Inasmuch as the Lutheran confession binds the church exclusively to the apostolic gospel, it frees the church from allegiance to all other teaching which is not grounded in God's Word.

The apostolic gospel includes a direct backward reference to the content of the Holy Scriptures of Israel. The apostolic gospel cannot properly be proclaimed where this reference to the Old Testament does not occur. How this is to be fulfilled and what its dogmatic relevance is cannot be further developed here. We must be satisfied simply with the assertion that the apostolic gospel as such witnesses to the peculiar dogmatic authority of the Old Testament regarding just this gospel. The manner in which the Holy Scriptures of Israel have their authority in the Church of Jesus Christ is fundamentally different from that which they enjoy in the synagogue. But the authority of these Scriptures is not abrogated by the gospel. Rather, it is incorporated within the gospel itself and determined by the gospel in its uniqueness. Even if, according to our present knowledge, the theological forms in which the apostolic message points back to the Old Testament can no longer be considered identical with those forms employed by the New Testament, we today must still protect the essential matter intended with these forms. The reference to the Old Testament incorporated within the apostolic gospel places the Christ-event in the concrete history of God's salvatory action. This began already in the creation, was carried forth in the election of Israel with its decisive bent toward Messianic fulfillment, and moves on toward its culmination in the Day of the Lord. His Lordship dare never be separated from His Messiahship. This is the deepest ground for the gospel's Old Testament reference and for the peculiar authority of the Old Testament in the Church of Jesus Christ as testified to by the gospel itself. Therefore, the apostolicity of the apostolic gospel cannot be protected if its self-professed tie-up with the Old Testament as Holy Scripture is surrendered.

The apostolic gospel is given to us in the New Testament writings. This sentence appears to be self-evident. In truth, it is even more difficult to establish than the authority of the Old Testament. The apostolic gospel is not written letters, but the living Word. The apostolic gospel is the kerygmatic witness of a sharply bounded circle of persons. In the dogmatic sense of the word, "apostles" are the eye-witnesses of the resurrected Lord who were appointed as witnesses by the resurrected Lord himself on the occasion of His Easter appearances. Paul, who first saw the resurrected Lord after Pentecost and was sent out by Him, had to fight for the recognition of his apostolic office. The church at all times has recognized the apostolic authority of Paul. Besides Paul, there is the company of twelve contemporary apostles who represent an institution of the last age. We do not know whether still other disciples saw the resurrected Lord and were commissioned as His messengers. The apostolic gospel is the message of salvation and the teaching of salvation which those authorized eyewitnesses proclaimed. But where do we take hold of this apostolic gospel? It appears to be an irony of history that we do not have with certainty any written word from the eleven or twelve, but

only from the one who called his an untimely birth. What is the relation of the other writings of the New Testament which do not stem
with certainty from Paul to the apostolic gospel? What is the relation
of the other New Testament writers to the Apostles? And in what
relation are the accepted and worked-over traditions which are in the
New Testament and the proclamation and teaching of the Apostles?

When we, together with the Formula of Concord, declare the New
Testament writings to be the apostolic writings, we affirm that the
Scripture stands for us in the place of the oral apostolic gospel. With
what right do we do this? What kind of assertion is this? Certainly
this is not a purely historical judgment, even if historical considerations
play their role. Is it not the conviction that the apostolic gospel given
to us in the New Testament writings is the fundamental confession of
the church? No one today can repeat the doctrines of inspiration in
the sixteenth and seventeenth centuries in order to establish the
dogmatic authority of Holy Scripture. From what source, then, do
we establish the dogmatic authority of the New Testament part of
Holy Scripture? Are the theologians today really in a position still
to speak of Holy Scripture as "the sole rule and standard according
to which all dogmas together with all teachers should be estimated
and judged"? Does the Lutheran Church still have a rule and
standard over dogma and teacher in its midst? Especially in regard
to the New Testament this question strikes me as particularly distressing. Yet allegiance to the Lutheran confession today entails just
this affirmation that the New Testament, as a collection of writings
in which the apostolic gospel is given to us from the mouths of the
authorized eyewitnesses of the resurrected Lord, is the only fully
decisive norm for the transmission of this gospel.

I hold the dogmatic establishment of this sentence to be an
urgent task for a theology bound to the Lutheran confession. We
dare not close our eyes to the fact that the concrete authority of Holy
Scripture has also disintegrated to a large extent in our church and
in the theology taught in our church. When the question is posed
concerning the content which our sermons and instruction must have
in order to be the saving Word of God's gospel, many other judges
alongside of, or in evasion of, the Scriptures are cited, if indeed
the absolutely fundamental conviction that the salvation of men
before God is given by God to men in Word and sacrament has not
itself already been contested. In order to find the content of the gospel's proclamation, men appeal variously to a definite pious experience, or to a certain understanding of existence, or to a modernistic

interpretation of the *justificatio impiorum,* or to a minimal reduction of the gospel given in Scripture to an arbitrary stipulation of "what relates to Christ." The consequence of this is that in the name of a so-called text criticism, large parts of the New Testament are robbed of their concrete authority for the proclamation and teaching of the church (e.g., Luke, Acts, and the so-called Deutero-Pauline and the Pastoral Letters). The teaching content of these writings is already considered by many to be a sign of the apostasy of the early church to Catholicism. In place of a multiplicity of witnesses, many speak of contradictory opposition. Even if we do not consider the twilight area of the New Testament canon—the *Antilegomena,* deuterocanonical writings—and limit ourselves to that part of the canon uncontested by the Lutheran Reformation, even there many no longer see the unity of the New Testament witnesses in their diversity and their diversity in unity. They see, rather, in the core of the canon itself, a mutually exclusive contradiction. But if the New Testament no longer holds together, if in the canonical books of the New Testament there is no longer a consensus understood regarding the proclaimed gospel, then any confessional loyalty is likewise fundamentally impossible. To the degree to which the church loses the concrete authority of Holy Scripture, it loses also a binding consensus in regard to the content of the proclamation of the gospel. In place of confessional allegiance, loyalty to this or that theological opinion steps forward with the professed exclusive authority of a dogma. Whenever Scriptural authority is lost, the *Confessio* of the church is replaced by the heresies of the schools.

In the last 250 years, the Lutheran Church has not been able to overcome the theological crises through which it has had to pass. It is still largely unaware of the depth of its plight. All talk of confessional allegiance is meaningless, if Holy Scripture is lost as the concrete judge over all proclamation and teaching. The confession presupposes Scripture, and Scripture not as an historically given phenomenon, but as a speaking authority! This presupposition has become problematic for many pastors, theologians, and non-theologians. For this reason, confessional loyalty has also become problematic. Loyalty to the Lutheran confession today entails, in the very first instance, a recapturing of the presupposition behind every confessional fidelity; namely, the concrete authority of the canonical Scriptures of the Old and New Testaments for the content of the proclamation of the gospel and the administration of the sacraments.

We can also formulate this presupposition behind every confessional allegiance as follows: the churches, the congregations, its shepherds, and teachers hear with great unanimity the voice of the Good Shepherd in the voices of His messengers from the canonical writings of the Bible. The listening to the speaking Bible, the hearing of the unanimously harmonious voices of the Scriptural witnesses, the self-revelation of the Word of God in the Scripture through the work of the Holy Ghost: this is the presupposition necessary for Scripture to exercise its judging office over all teachers and teaching in the church. When the congregations, their shepherds, and teachers are not given to hear the saving Word of the gospel in a greater harmony within the totality of Holy Scripture—instead, perhaps, of a condensed Paul—then the stability of the church itself is in danger. Then the confessing Word of the church becomes impossible; its loyalty to a confession becomes a formal, juridical affair. If Holy Scripture no longer speaks out of its canonical breadth and depth as the living Word of God to the congregations, its shepherds, and teachers, then any possible binding upon a confession is precluded from within and becomes meaningless.

Allegiance to the Lutheran confession today means a recognition of the deep spiritual crisis in our church which consists of the fact that the speaking Scripture, the judging Scripture, the Scripture as sole rule and standard for proclamation and doctrine, has largely been lost. Confessional loyalty today must include, above all, a prayer for the coming of the Holy Spirit who will once again permit us to hear the apostolic voices and the apostolic authority inherent in the united Old and New Testaments.

When this happens, and in the degree to which it happens, it will become clear to us that loyalty to the Lutheran confession today also means loyalty to the confession of the early church. To illustrate this in only one, however decisive, point: It is impossible to confess the justification of the sinner if Jesus of Nazareth is not truly God. In this knowledge that Jesus is true God, born of the Father in eternity, and also true man, born of the Virgin Mary, we may see the center of the early church confessions. One cannot confess the *homoousios* of the Nicene Creed, however, without confessing the Trinitarian doctrine of the Athanasian Creed. Do I go too far in saying that our position in regard to the confessions of the early church will be decisive not only as to whether we know ourselves to be bound to the Lutheran confession, but also, simultaneously, as to whether we are truly protecting the apostolic gospel in our midst? Calling attention to "the results of New Testament exegesis" in no way repudiates this assertion. Exegetically, the facts of the case here are unequivocal. No one contests that the Pauline and Johannine, as well as the breadth of the other New Testament Scriptures, represent a Christology of pre-existence. To be sure, as compared with the Fathers of the Reformation, we have become very clever through our historical-critical Biblical research. We can work out the finest nuances between the interpretations of the pre-existence of Christ in the genuine Pauline letters, the Deutero-Pauline works, and the Gospel of St. John. We can exhibit with virtuosity the relation of this idea to other conceptions in the history of ideas and in the history of religions. But the central question remains whether that which John 1, Phil. 2, and Heb. 1 witness of Christ is true, as testified to by Luther, the Lutheran confession, and essentially, the Reformed confession. The question still remains for us as to whether or not the Scriptural witness to the incarnation of the Son of God is true, or only a form of presentation which merely brings to expression the Jesus-event's significance inasmuch as it is left to my interpretation at my discretion. The ultimate question still remains undecided after all the clever and careful exegesis is concluded.

It is uncontestable that Matthew and Luke testify that Jesus was not conceived from human seed, but was conceived by the Holy Ghost, and therefore was born of the Virgin Mary. In view of this statement in the Gospels, no serious exegetical problem lies before us. But to which theologian does this statement of the gospel witness still speak as an apostolic witness to Christ? The confession of the Virgin Birth of Jesus Christ is not concerned with a *sacrificium intellectus,* but rather solely with a Spirit-worked insight into the gospel content of this statement, with the Spirit-worked knowledge of the God-ordained indicatory character of these circumstances. Are we clear, however, that we never have an indication without the thing that indicates?

Or should I point to the resurrection of Jesus which also comprehended and transformed His corporeality, or to the externality of His Easter appearances which are never understood in the New Testament as spiritual visions, or to the coming apocalyptic end of the world and the return of Jesus to judge the living and the dead? Each time the exegetical situation as such is quite clear, but its appropriation into modern theology, and its affirmation as a dogmatically valid assertion, are equally contested. This is once again a sign indicating to what extent the speaking Scripture, the judging Scripture, the Scripture as a concrete norm, has been lost. It is also a sign showing what allegiance to the Lutheran confession would mean today if this fidelity really were what its nature demands, namely, loyalty to the apostolic witness of Christ in the Holy Scripture.

Contemporary binding to the Lutheran confession entails the realization that the retention of the dogma of the early church by the Reformation is not merely a halfway stop, intelligible from historical considerations, but rather belongs necessarily to the content of the gospel itself. Lutheran confessional loyalty today means the insight that the reality of the forgiveness of sins is radically questioned, if Jesus is not true and essential God, Son of the eternal Father, of one substance with the Father, and true and essential man, born of the Virgin Mary, of the same substance as man, only without sin. Binding to the Lutheran confession today means the obligation to draw the necessary relation between the content of the apostolic gospel and the dogma of the early church.

I come now to the specifical Reformation content of the Lutheran confession. In no point will the Lutheran confession establish a new dogma. Indeed, the church cannot establish new articles of faith. It can only witness to the faith content of the Scriptures of the prophets and apostles already given through God's revelation. At the very outset, the Lutheran confession repudiates any "new" doctrine even within the limitations of this church's witness to the Bible's faith content. The gospel did not disappear in the year 120 and then reappear in Wittenberg in the years 1516-1521. The gospel had its witnesses of truth in all ages: under the hay, straw, and feathers of the dear Church Fathers, and in the Roman Church itself, as Art. XXI of the *Confessio Augustana* assures us at the end of its first part. According to the Lutheran confession, the *ecumenical grounding* of a doctrine speaks for its loyalty to Scripture; the peculiar novelty of a doctrine does not! It is often too disquieting for us to see how concerned Luther was to formulate no doctrine which could be branded as "new" in the history of Christian thought. Certainly his understanding of the New Testament texts in question was decisive for the doctrine of the real presence of the body and blood of Christ in the Sacrament. But of great comfort to him was the fact that he knew himself to be at one with the Fathers here. Think how freely Melanchthon quotes from the Canon of the Mass in the Eastern Church: *in quo aperte orat sacerdos, ut mutato pane ipsum corpus Christi fiat*

[95]

(Apol. X). From this viewpoint, the Lutheran confession is an irenic confession, a peacemaking confession, a brother seeking confession, an ecumenically responsible, and thereby, catholic confession. Confessional allegiance today must also incorporate the obligation to bring an ecumenical breadth to our theology whereby we seek the gospel witness in Patristics, in the Orthodox Church, even in the Roman Church. We dare not pay homage to a narrowly gauged Luther re-pristination which limits itself essentially to a one-sided selection from the writings of the so-called "Young Luther."

It is precisely because of this ecumenical grounding that the Lutheran confession also shows polemical acumen. The Lutheran No to the church of the pope has as its presupposition a Yes to the catholic church and the apostolic gospel. And this gives power to its rejection of the papal church. Loyalty to the Lutheran confession today means the obligation to repeat from these same grounds the same No to the contemporary papal church with its *Vaticanum* and its dogmatizing of *assumptio Mariae virginis*. Why is the Protestant protest against Rome often so ineffective, so weak, and in such small measure convincing? This is precisely because the necessary preconceptions are often lacking upon which the Lutheran confession based its No to Rome. Whoever says No to the papal church on the basis of having torn a single element out of the gospel as given in Scripture and transmitted in the *ecclesia catholica,* gives thereby a distorted witness. Such a polemic is irrelevant; it does not meet the papal church, and serves only to strengthen it indirectly. Only where the No to Rome is spoken out in the name of the apostolic and catholic church in the power of a Biblical gospel is it really being confronted. Everything else is but a sham battle which can only serve to drive earnest Christians into the arms of Rome.

Loyalty to the apostolic gospel, and thereby, rootage in the universal Christian Church, also necessitates the inner Protestant polemics of the Lutheran confession against the enthusiasts and the sacramentarians. This No has nothing to do with a medieval, immature theological opinion, but rather with the permanency of the catholic church, which as such is the church of the apostolic gospel. There can only be *one* ground for the Lutheran Church to revise its confession at this point: If the apostolic witness of Holy Scripture regarding the function of the *verbum externum* and the nature of baptism and Holy Communion would today teach us something different from that which the fathers of the Lutheran confessions have understood of them, then we must revoke the *damnant* of Art. V and the *improbant* of Art. X of the Augsburg Confession.

In answering this present question, it is fundamental for the Lutheran confession, as for us, that the witness of Scripture legitimately takes the place of the original apostolic witness. If we compare Paul's understanding of Holy Communion in 1 Cor. 10 and 11 with that of Matthew, Mark, and Luke, then modern exegetical studies have probably made the point quite clearly that for Paul, as for Mark, to name only this oldest witness—the blessed bread and cup are carriers of the body and blood of Christ. The exegetical problem arises here only when we are concerned with the meaning of the historical tradition which stands behind the New Testament texts on Holy Communion. We have no cause to protest when men attempt to illuminate this historical tradition. But we do have cause to protest when they attempt to emphasize the more or less hypothetically reconstructed historical tradition in opposition to the Holy Communion witness of St. Paul and the gospel writers. This dogmatizing historicism in New Testament exegesis means fundamentally nothing less than attacking the efficacy of the Spirit of Christ in this history of tradition. This dogmatizing historicism means fundamentally nothing less than attacking the foundation upon which the catholic and apostolic church stands or falls; namely, that the concrete form of the Scriptural witness itself—and not the postulation of a previous stage of tradition—is the source for the concrete apostolic authority against which all teachers and teachings of the church are to be judged. If we view the concrete Scripture witness itself, however, there is every cause for withstanding every softening of the known teachings of the fathers in Articles V and X of the Augsburg Confession in the name of the catholic and apostolic church.

The situation is not different when we view the doctrine of predestination in the Reformed confession. There are many points with which issue must be taken. Yet the decisive point appears to me to be the universal significance of the salvatory work of Christ. If the teaching of predestination in the Gallican Confession and its relatives is valid, then Christ has not died for all men, but only for a part of humanity, for those elect from eternity. From this standpoint, the Helvetic Formula of Consensus (1625) justifiably dogmatized the frightful sentence that on the grounds of the eternal fatherly decree, Christ has been made warrant of the New Covenant only for the elect. For the same reason, only because of them and not for all men who will be born, did Christ take upon himself His bitter death.

[97]

The gospel also compels us to follow the decision of the fathers of the Lutheran Confessions in the matter of the presence of Jesus in His Church. It belongs to the soteriological center of the gospel itself that we proclaim that Jesus Christ is truly with His own "not only according to His divinity, but also according to and with His assumed human nature, by which He is our Brother and we are flesh of His flesh." The response which the Heidelberg Catechism gives to this matter under the famous Question 47 is not merely a "theological working accident" (Karl Barth), but goes right to the heart of the gospel itself. Behind it stands a theological conception which is of decisive significance for church and Spirit, Word and sacrament. On the other hand, the exegetical situation is quite clear: He to whom all power has been given in heaven and on earth, He who is raised above all heaven and yet fulfills all in all, is precisely the man Jesus who is ordained as Lord of all powers.

Also in the teaching on church order, the Lutheran Confessions guard the knowledge that only one office is divinely instituted in the church, the office which administers the means of grace. Everything else in church order is to serve this office and to be ordered in the freedom of faith on the ground of its insight according to the standards of what is fitting and suitable. An extension of the *iure divino* for the validity of the church's order—as the confessions of the Reformed Church demand—is to be repudiated in the name of the freedom for which Christ has set us free.

Loyalty to the Lutheran confession also affords some clear direction for the Lutheran churches' attitude within the ecumenical movement. They dare not allow the ecumenical movement to try to effect a Protestant synthesis on some mediating line among the teachings of Baptists, Methodists, Calvinists, and Lutherans, together with an acceptance of the Anglican episcopal system of government, as if this would provide a unifying principle under whose sheltering roof all could gather together when no clarity and agreement have been won on the truth of the gospel. This is not because we hold that the Lutheran Confessions of the 16th century must be rigidly retained at any cost in the current ecumenical discussion, but because of our concern for the proper retention of the apostolic gospel of Holy Scripture.

Up to now we have been looking outward. Now we must turn to our own doors. What does fidelity to the Lutheran confession mean today for the inner life of the Lutheran churches themselves? I recall first what Lutheran confessional loyalty does *not* mean: not a *sacrificium intellectus,* not a servile submission to a doctrinal law as under the rod of a tyrannical master, not a juridical handling of statutory letters; but also not a formal juridical act in which the content of the teaching and proclamation receives no significance. Loyalty to the Lutheran confession is much more a gift than something which can be forced upon someone who is not already prepared from elsewhere to do so. Loyalty to the Lutheran confession is a gift of the Holy Ghost, over which no man can decree with his own power. Loyalty to the Lutheran confession is the spiritual insight into the harmony between the gospel which manifests itself as the living Word of Holy Scripture and the confessional assertions of the fathers. Loyalty to the Lutheran confession is an act of spiritual freedom for which we can be freed alone by the power of the gospel given to us by the Holy Spirit.

When this kind of confessional loyalty comes to the fore, it is not accomplished by a mere recitation of the formulations of the fathers. When the insight breaks through that the apostolic gospel has come to legitimate expression in the Lutheran confession, and particularly in its theologically controversial sections, then the confession exercises its concrete authority as *norma normata* in the church. For the apostolic gospel itself practices its authority through the confession. But the authority of the apostolic gospel is always concrete; it demands decision. In its presence one cannot remove oneself into a sphere of amiable detachment. Should the miracle occur that this spiritual fidelity to the Lutheran confession would come to pass in some Lutheran Church, there would simultaneously take place a great penitential movement in regard to doctrine, sermon, and administration of sacraments. Spirit-worked fidelity to the Lutheran confession would overcome the paralysis which the historicism of the last 200 years has exercised over theology and sermon. Where confessional fidelity takes place in the sense described here, one cannot proceed as if nothing has happened in theology and the history of ideas since 1700. Fidelity to the Lutheran confession today does not demand a formalistic recitation and repetition of the sayings of the fathers, but rather their responsible and actualized exposition and application. If we want to speak today of a genuine loyalty to the Lutheran confession, then we are obligated to address ourselves to the contemporary situation of the year 1957 in saying what we confess when we confess together with the fathers. Since the year 1580, the Lutheran Church has not ventured under the guidance of the Holy Spirit to reiterate or to explain in a binding fashion various of the theologically controversial articles of the Augsburg Confession for all of its congregations, shepherds, and teachers. There have been many opportunities to do this. Why did we remain silent? Dare we remain silent any longer? Between 1580 and 1957 lies the collapse of Protestant Orthodoxy; Pietism, the Enlightenment, Idealism, Historicism, and Existentialism—all have left their traces in the sermons of the church down to this day. When today we demand of every ordinand a Yes to the teaching of the Lutheran confession, without first telling him what binding content this Yes contains in our historical situation today, then we are either demanding too much, or else we are permitting him to interpret his Yes as he sees fit, since no one is in the position any more to declare in a binding fashion what this Yes includes in terms of concrete content. When the Lutheran Church does not dare to proclaim in a binding manner, at least in respect to some central content of the gospel which is the binding witness of the apostolic gospel as it was expressed on so many printed pages of its confessions, then it betrays the Spirit of God which wants to give its actualizing expositions now, today, here in our historical situation with the truth of the apostolic gospel. Fidelity to the Lutheran confession today, therefore, means a common agreement on an *Epitome* to the Lutheran confessions which applies the Biblical insights of the fathers to our contemporary situation, and simultaneously witnesses to and preserves the apostolic gospel against the heretical errors of our day.

Does this demand too much of us? What will our synods, bishops, and church leaders say to this demand? Would one not say, "That is a hot iron. We cannot touch it. The attempt to formulate an authoritative reiteration and explanation of the Lutheran confession by applying several articles of the Augsburg Confession to our contemporary theological and ecclesiastical situation, would create crisis after crisis. Because of the disposition of the church, such an attempt would precipitate disaster from the very outset. Therefore, we must not disturb the doctrinal twilight which lies over our church: Only in this twilight can we remain together."

Are those men right who speak in this fashion? Then only one alternative remains; the sigh out of the deep:

45114

Veni, Sancte Spiritus
et emitte caelitus
lucis tuae radium.

Veni, pater pauperum,
veni, dator munerum,
veni, lumen cordium . . .

Lava quod est sordidum,
riga quod est aridum,
sana quod est saucium.

The Confession as Gift and as Task

By Prof. Ernst Kinder

"Lutheran" implies loyalty of the church to the gospel and to the confessions which explicate the essence of the gospel, as these confessions have arisen out of the Lutheran Reformation.

OUR FIRST QUESTION is to ask ourselves: In what way, and with what right, do we call our church "Lutheran." This term does not connote the close tying of the church to the man Martin Luther with all his views and statements. That would be sectarian. The church derives its life from the redeeming and saving gospel of God originating in the Christ-event, and the church exists for the purpose of furthering this gospel. No man has said this more expressively than Luther. The Lutheran Reformation strove first to maintain that the gospel should occupy the central place in the church, and should be the guiding principle in all its doing, speaking, and organizing. That is what we mean when we say "Lutheran," for Luther gave expression to it more clearly and unequivocally than has any other man. It is a matter of the gospel, not Luther, as he himself so tirelessly pointed out.

There is however more to be said. The gospel is no mere subjective feeling, or a simple principle, but, on the contrary, it expresses itself in its own specific content. That the gospel is truly valid in the church, will not be simply postulated and maintained in general terms as such, but on the contrary, the gospel will be expressed by the church in all its essential fullness, in such a way as to be committed to the content of the gospel. That is confession.

In her confession, the church declares the gospel as that from which she derives her existence, and that for which she exists, the reality which is the basis of her being and the content of her duty and service. To this conception she binds herself as her rule of life and service. When we call ourselves Lutheran, it does not imply only the close connection of the church to the gospel, principally or in general, as Luther often drew our close attention to it, but rather, in addition, it also means the close connection of the church to the essential contents of the Confessions as expressions of the gospel. These confessions, which issued from the Lutheran Reformation, related as they were to the confessions of the Early Church, to Christ and to the Triune God, were again made known as confessions of the gospel.

In that the term "Lutheran" means both basically and essentially the confession of the church to the gospel, the word "evangelical" would be not only better but more appropriate. But regrettably, the word "evangelical" has come to mean in the passage of time a term for a general, indeterminate Protestantism without essential contents and norms, while on the other hand, the word "Lutheran" has become naturalized, and indicates the close tying up together of the gospel with a confessional statement. It is not a matter of terminology but of reality. And because this reality, namely the close connection of the gospel to the confession, is both important and essential to the life of the church, therefore I use the name "Lutheran" until such times as a better word presents itself, although it is neither a satisfactory nor happy choice of word.

Therefore, we now pose the question: Why must the church of the gospel have a confessional statement? What exactly does it mean that the church's confession has come *from* the gospel and points *to* the gospel?

II.

The confession is the response of the church to God's Word. It is its echo of faith to God's revelation of salvation. The church of the gospel cannot exist without this echo of faith, and cannot properly carry on its service to the gospel without it. Only by means of such an echo does the gospel make fruitful progress. Thus, even though the confession is not a constitutive factor it is still, however, the "conditio sine qua non" for the church of the gospel.

I said earlier that the church finds its life in the redeeming and saving Gospel of God for man, as that gospel happened in the Christ-event, and as it is basically and authoritatively witnessed in the Scriptures; also that the church exists for the purpose of purveying that gospel to man.

Now it is important that the gospel will not yield its further effects to man when conceived either in a mystical way, i.e. as a mere experience, or when conceived in a magical way, i.e. in an objective, automatic form as *opus operatum*. It will only achieve its full effect when seen as a *message* conveyed by faith in witnessing and preaching. This happens through personal conviction, through personal decision and response, namely through the medium of a person in such a way that it is consciously accepted, clearly understood, and decisively confessed. The gospel will be the source of the church's life and its norm of service, only in so far as the gospel is confessed by its faith essentially, and called by its name expressly. Otherwise it will not realize, either for the church, or through the church, the real purpose intended by God. It is in the nature of the gospel when conceived in terms of the *Word* of God that, though in its spiritual depth it goes beyond all human reason, and in the full intensity of its living dynamic it can never adequately be expressed in mere idea, nevertheless it is recognizable by its own distinctive categories, as Word, yes, the Word of truth, and will be so recognized and must be so recognized, without thereby being intellectualized. Thus it will not remain in the form of the inexpressible unknown. In that the gospel has been revealed in precise historical acts, and in a divine pattern, it is therefore expressible in terms of its own decisive lineaments.

Understood in this way, the confession resounds to the call of the gospel: the gospel is of such a nature that it will go forth to man as the Word of God in no other way than through the medium of the faithful confession of personal faith and of the congregation of the faithful.

The confession of the church consists not in leaving the gospel to work in a remote suspended state of animation as a monologue of God, but in giving response to it in an answer of faith as a sort of echo. It demands a positive response and a firm hold of the contents. Confession is the echo, the answer of the church to the saving revelation of God. The revelation of God, given in the form of the gospel, demands such an answer from faith and from the congregation of the faithful, and in fact evokes such a response itself. Without this response the church cannot exist in its relation to the gospel, nor can it rightly preach the gospel. To confess means the total commitment of a person, by which he stands or falls. In its confessional statements the church expresses the ground of its existence, and binds itself to this ground as its rule of life and guide to service in its preaching. In this way, the confession stands on the one hand between the saving revelation of God which gives the church its foundation, and on the other hand, the service and the development of the message for which purpose the church is there: between these, i.e., between revelation and preaching, confession exercises a necessary and indispensable function. By that it is clear that confession does not constitute the church. The church was constituted and is constituted through the gospel. But this gospel, which is to effect its work through the medium of the church, thereby demands the decision and the echo of the confession, and itself evokes this as a necessity of its further progress. The confession is not the first but the second word—it is *re-actio*. The first word is God's confession to us: He confesses himself to us men in Christ. Our salvation exists in this fact. But that must be personally accepted by us. God's confession to us will evoke our confession to Him and to His works and gifts as our echo of faith, and through our confession it will be further proclaimed. Revelation, faith, confession and preaching are a chain which permits of no broken link. We must see the confession as a necessary and indispensable link of the chain, in which faith and the church have their existence, their life and their mission. If the church would really be the church of the gospel, then it must be the church of a confession which points to its gospel.

III.

Genuine church confession is a confession of the essential and decisive subject matter of Holy Scripture. It arises out of the experience made in and by the church in its actual life with regard to and through the essential contents of Holy Scripture. The confession has no intrinsic value, and is not an end in itself. Rather it is to act as a guidepost to the "core and sum total" of the Holy Scripture—and therefore also as guidance for the church's service along the line of proper proclamation of the gospel to others. Therefore it must also constantly prove itself by the test of the Holy Scripture, as "Norma normans."

When confession is viewed in this way, as demanded by the gospel and evoked by the gospel itself, it cannot be considered as opposing the Biblical witnesses. Scripture and confession are not two differently based authorities which can be played over against one another, but they both originate in the same root, namely the gospel, and are both based on the one and the same gospel in a certain precise relationship: The Biblical witnesses are the authentic, canonical, original proof of the gospel as constitutive and normative; for faith's confession is the echo of faith both of the individual believer and of the community of the faithful. The essential content of both is the same, namely the gospel: first as the original conviction in God's name, and again as the echo of faith. The confession of the church is not merely a confession to anything or nothing but a confession to the central, decisive, factual content of the Scriptures! Confession confesses from the experience of faith, the center and the climax, the "core and sum total" of the diverse and numerous Biblical witnesses.

That Scripture and confession come from one and the same root finds clear expression in the fact that the first confessional statement of the church, a confession on which all other confessions of the church are based, was the determining of the New Testament Canon! Standing under the inner power of the gospel the early church professed the collection of the New Testament writings as its authentic and canonical foundational witness. The church had not begotten these writings, but they had begotten it. As an echo from the early church, the church adopted by name and committed itself to these writings from which it took the authentic, canonical gospel. The fixing and limitation of the New Testament canon was a confessional act in the strictest sense of the word. The principle, *sola scriptura,* is not a neutral premise prior to confession, but is already a confessional statement originating in the gospel, and intended for the right preaching of the gospel. All further real confessions of the church must be viewed essentially in the lines and in the pattern of this its first confession, seen as a basis and indeed a paradigm.

In contradistinction to the Greek Orthodox or the Roman Catholic Church, we see the church's confession not as revelation itself or as fulfillment and further development of the Scriptures on the same level, but rather, in the other dimension of *echo* and *answer* to revelation! Indeed, we could say that it has its own necessary place and indispensable significance precisely in this functional context.

From the outset the church could not confine itself to the formal limitation of the canon of the first witnesses of the gospel. But at the same time it indicated the inner unity of the Biblical matter, expressed as it is in its various forms. In the confessions of the church the principle, "according to the Scripture," is not only mainly demanded and asserted, but here it is really practiced and effected in calling by name particularly what the substantial and decisive content of the Scriptures is! In this way the confession supports the principle "according to the Scriptures"! The content is an appeal to Scripture rather than a mere formula which is not obligatory, and which says nothing in particular because it says everything in general. The formula, *sola scriptura*, is indeed, as said earlier, already a confessional statement itself issuing from the core of Scripture, the gospel. The formula therefore is valid, not in the sense of a neutral axiom, but only hand in hand with the essential confession of the Scriptures as the norm of faith and the goal of faith. The attempt must never be made to dissociate the formula *sola scriptura* from confession, and make it into a principle of Biblical exposition, for in this event there is legalistic Biblicism and a reversion to Fundamentalism. The so-called "Formalprinzip" of the Lutheran Reformation *(sola scriptura)* and the so-called "Materialprinzip" *(justification by faith)* belong together—you cannot have the one without the other!

The confession is also necessary for the prevention of perverse appeal to Scripture, when men claim its authority in a spirit other than that of the gospel. The church must dissociate itself from such activity. This it does by means of its confessional statements. The essential content of the phrase, "according to the scriptures," is not met by a simple appeal to the Bible as such, for all appeal to that authority, but it is met by an existential decision of faith. In this way, there is really no decisive confessional affirmation without its corresponding negation. But it must not be assumed that this antithetical, negative function of confession is primary. The primary function is much more positive, as we have seen. It is the echo of faith evoked and demanded by the gospel, without which the church of the gospel can neither exist nor function. And on this principle, the confession has its own critical and deciding function which for the sake of the truth of the gospel we must never disregard.

In relation to the Scriptures the confession has, therefore, no significance in itself, and no purpose of its own. It originates in an experience of the Scriptures in faith, in an existential experience within the church in relation to the Scriptures and with the Scriptures. In times of uncertainty, i.e., when it was a matter of the meaning of the fulness of the gospel for the church "to be or not to be," the church has presented a confessional statement as a pointer to the decisive center of Scripture, a pointer to its continuing message. And in this way, as the confessional statement has not taken on its existence from itself, therefore, it is not there for itself, but only as a means of helping towards the understanding of the central and decisive content of Scripture and to serve as a guide to the gospel. Confession is the living expression of the truth, when it is seen as coming from the experience of the substance of Scripture, in and through the medium of the confessional experience of a church and pointing back again to Scripture: indeed, "Scripture is its own interpreter," through the medium of an experience within the church. Confession indicates the basic obligatory preaching on the foundation of a scriptural experience—that abiding element in all real true preaching. Our preaching must be actually addressed to modern man, but it must be identical in its essence with the preaching of the apostles and prophets! It is this which the confessional statement sets forth. Without this, other principles as regulative for Scripture interpretation and preaching would of necessity creep in; for the church needs some sort of regulative principle between revelation and preaching, and indeed always has some such principle: we cannot be neutral and without presuppositions in relation to the Scripture! A pure presuppositionless Biblicism is self-deception! Every man has in this respect, whether it is manifest or hidden, known or unknown, certain guiding principles, and, when they are not those of the church, then they are those of a philosophy, of a "Weltanschauung," of a limited subjectivity, of the spirit of the age, or of politics. Confession in the first place leads us to respect the experience of the church in the matter of Scripture in our own dealings with Scripture as responsible churchmen, and in the process to lead us further by means of it.

And as the confession originates in a central, substantial scriptural experience, and as it is there only to serve to an experience of the content of Scripture in its continued proclamation, thus it stands essentially under Scripture! In that it points us to Scripture, so does it always authenticate itself in every simple detail *in* Scripture! We do not possess a confession to observe and preserve it for its own sake, but only in a functional capacity in relation to Scripture and the preaching of the church. This is really its true nature. We have to conduct the living exchange between confession and Scripture in the established manner. It is possible to preserve confessions in a static way, but they must be used and applied! And in their very nature they will be used as directives to the Scripture! A signpost has no worth or value in itself, but only as a guide. In so far as we treat the confession as guide to Scripture, and from that as serving for a guide to preaching and the handling of the sacraments, and with this intention practice and further it, in this sense only can it prove and authenticate its rightness, truth, and genuineness. In this way we can say something essentially true about confession, if we practice it in the spirit and for the purpose for which it alone exists, namely in relation to Scripture and from Scripture to preaching; and not only practice it but also in so doing authenticate it. It is, therefore, senseless and useless, as so often happens today, merely to speak of a confession in and for itself, whether it be for or against the confession. There is no such thing as a confession in and for itself, or a confession as a principle. There are only certain concrete, precise confessional statements, and it only gives sense and purpose when we speak of confession as meaning concrete, particular, precise statements in relation to Scripture and preaching. Only in this way does confession justify its rightness and its validity. Therefore only such arguments for or against confession are worthy and to be taken seriously, which refer to its precise statements in relation to Scripture and in relation to the church's message.

IV.

The confession is not to exist in the church as something static; rather it needs to be activated in the church—and this, in the direction of gospel and Holy Scripture, as well as in the direction of the life and proclamation of the church. In such an activation one must always keep the confession in its functional and instrumental organic connection to both sides. If one tears the confession loose from this connection and raises it to the level of something absolute, then a false confessionalism results, which cannot help but use the good and important gift of the confession in an incorrect, and for the church disastrous, way.

It is now clear in what way the confession is to be understood as an important and indispensable gift of God originating in the gospel and directed to the church, a gift which cannot be neglected or despised without serious harm.

The real confessions of the church were not subtly worked out by theological professors, or made by ecclesiastical politicians considering only expediency, but they are given to the church by God. They are given to the church by God in her historic experience of the Scripture, and she is entrusted with them as an instrument to realize the knowledge of the revelation of God and to proclaim it. A church that is truly evangelical cannot without serious hurt to itself despise or dispense with these confessions. It is indeed of its very nature and content, and neither a claim by itself nor an assumption of Protestantism, that the gospel is the heart of the entire Scripture for the church and its marching orders.

It is at once clear in what way the gospel is a task calling the church today. In that the confession is a gift to us, it is a responsibility entrusted to us. The confession is essentially a call to service. Originating in the scriptural experience of the Fathers, it is presented to us. But as such it has no sense and purpose merely in itself, but only in so far as it calls us now to our own obligation. We respect the confessions as gifts from God only in so far as we use them rightly and, in the way intended by the gospel, put them to their intended use. Thus we cannot and indeed must never be content with the mere historical and ecclesiastical possessions of the confessions as such. Man cannot hold a confession statically, that would be a contradiction in terms, but only receive it as a present, and wholeheartedly prosecute that to which it calls. A confession in its real nature is a matter not of possession but of obligation.

The first task to which the confessions call is that we know, really know, the contents in each and every detail; further—that we take seriously their claim to be a witness of the central and decisive content of Scripture; that we allow ourselves to be driven back through the statements of the confession to the Scriptures and carefully allow the confessions to be checked and proved true by Scripture; that we bring together confession and Scripture in their proper juxtaposition and in a living interchange of ideas. In such an exchange the Scripture reveals its true meaning and verifies the confession, and thereby we are enabled to assent to the confessional statement as our own personal confession to the gospel. If this is not done, then the confession can neither be rightly confessed nor properly used. If we wish to gain and to maintain a right relationship to the confession, then we must *constantly strive* to perform this prime task set us by the confession. Only in the right *use* of the confession, in the attempt to make effective its essential statements both with regard to the Scripture and with regard to the preaching can man gain its grasp of truth and its unique significance. Thus the confession presents us, its responsible confessors, with the task of using and realizing the confession in its true sense.

The right use of a confession consists in always keeping it in its living context and in the position between gospel and Scripture on the one hand and the life and the preaching of the church on the other hand. From this starting point the confession must be applied to oneself, to the life and mission of the church. It is not a matter of the worth of a confession but rather its real, vital application in the realms of preaching, the strengthening of faith, and pastoral and other work of the church. Do we in fact really do that, or do we pay respect to an honorable relic preserved under glass? When one really makes a vital application of the confession in the way described, then one first notices the rich, deep and living treasures that are contained in them: treasures not yet fully exhausted. We ought to speak not so much *about* the confession, but more happily to speak from it and to use it.

There is, however, a wrong use of the confession. Every misuse of the confession basically arises either from tearing it apart from its living, mediating function in relation to the gospel and the Scripture; or from tearing it apart from the life of faith and the preaching ministry of the church. This isolates it and makes it an end in itself. Then we have instead of a true confessional position, a false confessionalism, which though it makes much of the gift of the confession, nevertheless puts it to perverted use. To separate the confession from its true and vital relation to the gospel, and to make it an end in itself, is to make it into law and good works.

Misuses of the confession express themselves, for example, when one holds to the Lutheran confession simply out of mere traditionalism and conservatism, or from a purist legalism, or from stiffnecked self-will and Lutheran cavil, or even only to enhance Lutheran prestige and maintain the Lutheran concern. In this matter we must honestly prove to ourselves the real motives for our clinging to the Lutheran confession! Are we thinking of ourselves and our own security, or is it a matter of a response to the gospel? If we have in mind a concern for the situation and honor of the Lutheran Church, its prestige and security as a special preserve and as a particular church, then our loyalty to the confession is sectarian and legal, and is no longer a responsible service to the gospel!

Thus it happens that the very confession (in which we often take a somewhat pharisaic pride), by what it proclaims, most often summons us ourselves to come and confess. It is not *that* there is a relation of the confession to the Scriptures and to the present-day service of the church, but *what* that relation essentially is. The genuine Lutheran standpoint is not an anxious safeguarding of one's own position, but witness, positive working and service with what has been specially given to us and entrusted to us by God.

Just because we are convinced that in the confessional statements of the Lutheran Reformation the gospel is clearly shown as the real, true and decisive essence of the Scriptures, and indeed is there described as centrally and comprehensively as nowhere else, therefore we have a responsibility and a service to the whole Christian Church. From this task and responsibility we must never withdraw to become a particular church sufficient in itself. The distinguishing feature of the Lutheran confession does not lie in a claim to possess distinctive Christian truths, but rather in the resolute demonstration and the determined penetration to what is the very *center* of the whole, and what is thereby important for the whole. Seen in this light, the Lutheran Church is no church of a particular kind, but aims at the one holy catholic apostolic church, because in its confessions the center is clearly set out, knowingly, illuminating and dominating the whole. In this way we bear an ecumenical responsibility in our confessions. We ought, therefore, to pay serious attention to the confessions of other churches and in the light of the Scriptures as brothers grapple earnestly for the truth of the gospel. This we should do fully accepting our confessions, and in this pledge allow our confessions to prove themselves.

False Lutheran pride and self-sufficiency is only the reverse side of a false Lutheran inferiority complex. These show lack of confidence in the God-given responsibility of a confession, as well as an unhappy uncertainty.

Finally, it would be a false use of the confession, if we were so to look at it as if it held captive the gospel in its various points, as if we had the gospel guaranteed and contained in it (as if to say we had a "potted" gospel), as if we could go around with it in a literal, legal, and causistic fashion, as we would with a recipe book, or a book of laws. In this way the confession would be intellectualized, rationalized and thereby legalized, while in reality it is an echo from the gospel and should serve the purposes of the gospel. The gospel itself never permits itself to be strictly expressed by confessional statements and dogmas, but confessional statements and dogmas serve only to point to the gospel and provide a normative meaning for its preaching. We must never neglect this twofold significance of the confession: its significance as proof, and its significance for service. The confession points the way, and we must respect and not despise it. But in this basic direction we must first ourselves, in our own responsibility, have performed the living service to the gospel in the present situation. The confession does not in itself relieve the church of its responsibility of conveying its message to the world as it is today: it serves only to further it.

Conclusion

Thus we stand between a wrong despising of the confession on the one hand, and a wrong adherence to the confession on the other; between a false relativism and a false absolutism. The question is, which of the two dangers is the greater and the graver today? That may be answered differently in different lands and different churches, and one is obliged to stress one more than the other according to the real situation and its real demands. But, what is always true, we must view the confession from the starting point of the gospel and in relation to its service to the gospel. Only from this starting point and in reference to it must one see not only the serious, essential necessity and indispensability of the confession for the church, but also its functional, instrumental, indicative, regulative significance for its ministry. A perverted isolation of the confession, or turning it into an absolute, the hardening of it or the over-emphasizing of it, indeed all forms of false confessionalism will not be conquered by making relative, minimizing, or evading the confession, but only by making a positive, better use of it, on the lines argued. We shall make good progress not through an external relative modification of the confession but by its inner fulfillment. And this holds good not only within the Lutheran Church, and in the problems of confessions within the Lutheran Church, but in the problems of confessions within the ecumenical movement. We must view our confessional and ecumenical responsibility not in competition with one another, but the one through the other.

What Does Lutheran Confessional Allegiance Mean Today?

BY PROF. RERIN PRENTER

THE QUESTION BEFORE us can best be answered by means of addressing ourselves to two subsidiary questions. First, what does the actually operating allegiance to the Lutheran confessions really mean in our church today? Secondly, what kind of confessional allegiance is demanded from the content of the Lutheran confessions themselves?

There are two reasons why both these questions cannot be handled together. In the first place, we dare not uncritically accept the confessional allegiance which actually prevails in our church as if it were an infallible and unalterable arrangement which was valid for all time. If the confessions are really to be binding—that is, authoritative for the thought and action of our church—then the way in which we actually permit the confessions to become authoritative must constantly be tested against the content of the confessions themselves. In the second place, the different Lutheran churches all have a common Lutheran confession. But they share no unified interpretation and practice in regard to this confessional loyalty. If our theme is to treat different Lutheran churches in common, the proposed subsidiary questions must be dealt with separately.

We will treat the second question first. In a strict sense, the Augsburg Confession is the Lutheran confession. As we handle this major question of principle, the Augsburg Confession will be treated as representative of all the Lutheran confessions. We do not thereby overlook the fact that most Lutheran churches also include other Symbolical books among their Lutheran confessional documents. This fact will be of importance later when we consider the other question. However, as long as we now remain with this fundamental inquiry into the manner of confessional allegiance in the light of the content of the Lutheran confessions themselves, we can best serve our purpose by staying with the original, indeed classical, formulation of the Lutheran confessions.

In the Preface, the Augsburg Confession is called "our confession of faith," and what is meant by this is developed in the following words: "What manner of doctrine from the Holy Scriptures which has been up to this time set forth in our lands, dukedoms, dominions, and cities, and taught in our churches." In these articles of faith presented to the emperor at the Diet of Augsburg, the Protestants used the term "confession" in a definitely churchly context. In the church the proclamation of the Word of God proceeds from the texts of Holy Scripture. In these articles of confession, the content is summarily characterized as the proclamation of God's Word as derived from Scripture. And these articles are described as a confession of faith. In the Latin rendering, an important word is used: . . . *et nostram confessionem, cuiusmodi doctrinam ex scripturis sanctis et puro verbi Dei hactenus illi apud nos tradiderint. Tradiderint*—the proclamation of the Word of God, therefore, has the character of *tradition*. It consists in the faithful transmission of the trusted message of Holy Scripture to the congregation. This oral proclamation in the continually new transmission of the Biblical message is the confession of the church.

We see here how the elements, Scripture, proclamation, faith, and confession belong together. The message of Scripture must be proclaimed or else there would be no message. The proclamation occurs in the church, in the worship of the congregation. The proclaimed message finds faith in the church. The faithful congregation transmits the message it has heard from Scripture in its confession to all who have not yet heard, and thereby testifies in which form it heard the message. In a certain sense, the proclamation stands between Scripture and confession. It derives its total content from Holy Scripture. It does not do this, however, in a self-willed and unhistorical manner. The church in which the confessors of the Augsburg Confession teach is no Biblicistic sect, but is rather—as strongly stressed in the confession itself—the one catholic church, the church of the Fathers. This means that the confessors are willing to be led in their exposition of Biblical texts by the Fathers who had proclaimed this same message long before they had. This does not mean that "tradition" is placed above Scripture as a second source of knowledge. For the tradition is nothing more than the transmission of the message of the prophetic and apostolic Scriptures themselves. The fact then that the exposition of Scripture takes place together with the confession of the Fathers means that the texts of the Bible in the proclamation of the church are not to be interpreted as documents of universal truths, but rather as the witness to the mighty acts of God with His people, and through this people to all of mankind. This is a witness which is heard properly only in faith; that is, when one believes and acts in faith as if he belongs to the people for whom God's mighty deeds were intended. Therefore the confession of the congregation and Holy Scripture are inseparable wherever the message of Scripture is rightly proclaimed.

It is especially important to note in this connection that the congregation proclaims its confession not only in the sermon, but also far more in its baptism, Holy Communion, and free praise. Indeed, it must be asserted that here the confession comes to expression in its original form as the common confession of the gathered congregation in fixed, unalterable words. So the early church confessional "Symbols" have their "life-situation" in baptism and Holy Communion. When we say that someone preaches in accord with the confession of the church as he proclaims the message of Scripture to the congregation, we do not mean thereby that they hear something substantially different in the confession from what they have already heard in the Scripture, for the confession adds nothing new to Scripture. Nor do we mean that the confession establishes only one single interpretation of the texts from the very outset, so that the preacher is no longer free to allow the texts themselves to speak to him. *That* would be a very disastrous kind of confessionalism, one which would surely lead to heresy. True confessional preaching, on the one hand, does not mean that the confession has told the preacher *what* he must hear in Scripture; the Biblical texts provide this themselves, and all that the confession's content has to say about the message of Scripture is to point back to the Biblical texts. On the other hand, it does mean that the preacher is told *how* he should hear; namely, as one who has become a member of the body of Christ in baptism, and who has become united with Christ through the gift of His sacrificed body and blood in Holy Communion. As among those who are the property of Jesus Christ, and, through him, the people of God, he must hear the Biblical witness of God's deeds with His people in faith if he is properly to hear them at all. As an "observer" he could, to be sure, study these texts and try to explain them. But he could not proclaim and witness to their truth. There can be no talk of any conflict between confessional and Scriptural conformity in the sermon, for Scripture deals with God's mighty acts with His people and through them to all humanity, and the confession aims only at pointing back to this Scriptural witness. It reflects a basic misunderstanding when the words of the confession and the Scriptures are pitted against each other. The confession itself demands that we derive its meaning solely from Scripture. Nor can there be any talk of any substantial contradiction between the contents of the early church Symbols and the Augsburg Confession. Were such the case, it would have to be asserted that the confessional document was falsely, i.e. unscripturally, interpreted.

This can also be clearly observed from the construction of the Augsburg Confession. Its articles are only an exposition of the confessions of the early church in the light of Holy Scripture. For this reason, Art. 21 stresses that none of the preceding articles are in conflict with the teaching of the catholic church, indeed, the Roman Church. First, the chief articles concerning God and Christ are treated with their presupposition in understanding man as a lost sinner. Then follows the ministry of the church, and the means of grace. The articles treating special controversial matters such as free will, faith, and works, are developed in clear dependence upon the earlier fundamental articles.

Where a No, a *damnamus,* is spoken, it appears in order to mark the boundary between the one holy catholic church which knows itself united in the faithful hearing of the Biblical message by all its preachers and hearers, and all others with whom it cannot confess itself to be in unity because of a gospel different from the one which the one holy catholic church proclaims and transmits in, with, and under the exposition of the Biblical texts.

This interpretation of the relation between Scripture, proclamation, faith, and confession—as derived from the title "Confession" and its meaning in the Preface of the Augsburg Confession—is also made explicit in the articles contained within the confession proper.

> We limit ourselves to a few references in the following articles. Art. IV: "Also they [the Lutherans] teach that men cannot be justified before God by their own strength, merits, or works, but are freely justified for Christ's sake, through faith, when they believe that they are received into favor, and that their sins are forgiven for Christ's sake, who, by His death, has made satisfaction for our sins. This faith God imputes for righteousness in his sight." Art. V: "That we may obtain this faith, the Ministry of Teaching the Gospel and administering the Sacraments was instituted. For through the Word and Sacraments, as through instruments, the Holy Ghost is given, who works faith, where and when it pleases God, in them that hear the Gospel, to wit, that God, not for our own merits, but for Christ's sake, justifies those who believe that they are received into grace for Christ's sake." Art. VII: "Also they teach that one holy Church is to continue forever. The Church is the congregation of saints, in which the Gospel is rightly taught and the Sacraments are rightly administered. And to the true unity of the Church it is enough to agree concerning the doctrine of the Gospel and the administration of the Sacraments. Nor is it necessary that human traditions, that is, rites or ceremonies, instituted by men, should be everywhere alike."

Now we can answer the question: What *kind* of confessional allegiance is required by the content of this Lutheran confession itself?

1) *Who* binds here to the confession? It is the confession itself. It may sound strange, in and of itself, to speak here of an obligation. For the confession is an expression of faith, and faith, as a thankful hearing of the gospel, is an act of complete freedom. But just this freedom is an obligation, for the truth and the joy of the gospel binds our hearts to God. The confession binds our faith in freedom with the power of the truth in its witness to the gospel and nothing else.

(2) *How* is one bound to the confession? We are bound by the confession's fidelity to the message of Holy Scripture. The confession does not bind one to its own formulations, as if they were to provide an infallible and adequate theological presentation of what must be said today in the sermon. That would be to replace Holy Scripture with the confession which would be a grave falsification of its witness. A confessional sermon, for example, cannot be satisfied merely with not attacking the confession or by mechanically reproducing its sentences. It must rather proclaim to men *today* the message of Holy Scripture under the guidance of the confession. This may mean that other things will have to be said which were *not* so formulated in the

documents of the sixteenth century Lutheran Reformation, and that polemical formulations of that day may not simply be repeated in their peculiar form in our day. Central always is the *content* value, not theological slogans or opinions. The aim must always be genuine, contemporary proclamation, never reactionary repristination or restoration.

(3) *Who* is bound here? It is not only the preacher, but the whole congregation which is confessionally bound. For the confession is not only the concern of the preacher, since it does not come to expression exclusively in his sermon, but does so also in baptism and Holy Communion, and in the praise and prayer of the congregation. All who accept the confession are bound by it. It is important to maintain this observation when the question is raised regarding doctrinal discipline. The whole congregation, with the preacher of the gospel in particular, is bound through the confession to the truth of the gospel.

We may now proceed to our second question: What does the actually existing allegiance to the Lutheran confession really mean in my church? The question must be understood as follows: how is actual confessional allegiance related to the obligation which we have been discussing as set forth in the content of the confession itself?

(1) Confessional allegiance in the church can never be introduced and maintained by the force of the state. I consider as highly problematic the confessional fidelity required by the stipulations of the Danish-Norwegian King's Royal of 1655, whereby the King obligated all citizens to the one true religion as presented in the Unaltered Augsburg Confession of 1530, which was henceforth to be protected *by force* against all its enemies. In the confessing congregation, it is the gospel in the power of its truth which binds preacher and hearer to the confession. That, however, presupposes the absolute freedom of all men to permit themselves to be convinced solely by the truth of the proclaimed Word. I believe, therefore, that the Danish Constitutional Law of June 5, 1849, with its regulations for freedom of religion, etc., is more true to the intention of the Lutheran confession than any orthodox Lutheran sovereign church government. And what holds for a sovereign church government is valid, for it remains in the modern democratic church government (Volkskirchenordnung).

(2) Doctrinal discipline dare never be implemented by state church means. No civil authority may have the right to decide the question whether a preacher in conflict with the confession is correct

or not. Where people's churches exist, as in Scandinavia, which still have a certain state church government, this view must be stressed sharply to the state, even at the danger that doctrinal discipline will be menaced with less "effectiveness." And where—as in Denmark—there are still remains of the state church doctrinal disciplinary order, we must, I think, in fidelity to the confession, voluntarily desist from employing this civil authority to as great a degree as lies within our power, and attempt to settle doctrinal controversies in other ways within our own existing church order.

(3) Doctrinal discipline can only be exercised in a responsible fashion where there is real co-operation between the local congregation and the power of the bishop (using "bishop's power" here in the broadest possible sense as the right and duty of visitation which as a function can be performed by authorities other than the traditional bishop's office). Where the Lutheran confession is acknowledged, there can be no evangelical pope. The truth of the gospel is no secret wisdom. It is rather the clear content of the confession of the congregation which is known by every responsible member of the congregation. Once everything is explained in a doctrinal controversy, each member of the congregation must be able to act responsibly in the possible practice of doctrinal discipline. For neither a bishop nor a theological faculty is more infallible than the so-called laity. They also could one day be overcome by false teaching. On the other hand, because of the need for order and justice, doctrinal discipline dare never be carried out by the local congregation alone. The local congregation—or its representatives—must, however, be responsible for taking the initiative in every such case. The preacher, on the basis of his ordination vow, must be subject to being called to account for his proclamation. Certainly! But it is equally as important, that by virtue of this same ordination vow, each preacher be protected against any suspicious spying or church political intrigue in the practice of his office. He needs this protection especially whenever he proclaims the gospel in a new and unexpected way in true fidelity to the confession, and when, thereby, the representatives of traditional and beloved slogans and peculiar church political teachings consider themselves attacked. And he has a right to expect this protection from the administrator of the bishop's office. Unfortunately, church history is filled with many examples of cases where a great deal of theological error has been committed in the practice of doctrinal discipline, from the unjust judgment of Nestorius through the papal condemnation of Luther right down to our own day. This dare not lead to a

condition where the possibility and necessity of doctrinal discipline as such is attacked. It serves merely as a warning that such disciplinary proceedings in doctrinal controversies should be engaged in only in cases of dire necessity. Doctrinal discipline should only be practiced where a notorious heresy can be demonstrated, and then only after all alternative solutions to the conflict have been shown to be impossible. Furthermore, this notorious heresy, or open denial of the confession, can only take place where every responsible member of the congregation is able to detect this denial. In all other cases, it is not notorious heresy which is involved, but either a confusion not unbearable, or one of the many forms of the more or less clear doctrinal deviations. These dare not be equated with heresy, for in specific situations they may well bear a positive responsibility for the sake of a proper proclamation. As a concrete example, I name a group of the representatives of the so-called "demythologization program." This theology may well end up as notorious heresy. In its present uncertain and unfinished form, however, it cannot immediately be stamped as heresy and driven out with doctrinal disciplinary measures. Instead of this, it must first be earnestly discussed and carefully refuted without any thought of discipline in an atmosphere of free discussion. When doctrinal deviations, which are not yet notorious heresy, are too quickly treated as such with disciplinary action, then incalculable harm can be done. Yet it is against just this danger that we are protected by the confession. It should help us clearly to distinguish between the common faith of the church and our various theological opinions. Then we will never pose the unjust demand that all preachers of the church—in addition to their fidelity to the confession and the message of Holy Scripture which they assume in full responsibility under the guidance of the confession—should also proclaim our own special theological teachings. Unfortunately, such a demand has been made more than once in the past.

III

The Theology of Worship

The Sermon in the Lutheran Liturgy

By Prof. Conrad Bergendoff

1

THE SERMON IN LUTHERAN LITURGY is the result of a divine commission. It is the proclamation of a message which the Lord of the church has enjoined should be made known. "Go therefore and make disciples of all nations, baptizing them in the name of the Father and of the Son and of the Holy Spirit, teaching them to observe all that I have commanded you; and lo, I am with you always, to the close of the age." (Matt. 28:19, 20). The preacher may, like Jonah in the Old Testament, be reluctant to go, or like Paul in the New Testament, he may be on fire to make his message known. But neither the disposition of the messenger, nor the attitude of the recipients, determines the motive of the preacher. There is a Word of God which the nature of God determines is to be made known to men. Despite the weakness of the messenger, the opposition of those to whom it is addressed, or the difficulties to be overcome in making the Word known, the command is carried out. For the Word is not man's word, and the power by which it is made known is not man's power. The Spirit of God carries out His will and sends forth the messenger. "You did not choose me, but I chose you and appointed you that you should go and bear fruit and that your fruit should abide" (John 15:16).

For the Word is not merely a repetition of a fact, the announcement of a command or the declaration of a promise. It is in itself a creative and a judging Word. It has with it a power both to give life and to put to death. "For the Word of God is living and active, and sharper than any two-edged sword." (Heb. 4:12). Through the Word the Spirit of God is active in the hearts of men and leads to convictions of life and death. The Spirit convinces "the world of sin and of righteousness and of judgment" (John 16:8). In preaching the Spirit continues the speaking of Him who is the Word of God. "He will take what is mine," Christ said of the Spirit, "and declare it to you" (John 16:14). Men may accept the Word and find in it the truth of life or they may reject it and be condemned by its truth. But always it is God's Word that speaks to them. For God has not left the world which He has created and continues to create. Continually He speaks to the heart and mind, directing, illuminating, condemning, upholding, forgiving. Heaven and earth may pass away, "but the word of our God will stand forever." (Isa. 40:8).

2

The proclamation of the Word has created a community of believers who respond to the Word in a life of worship. They become a people of God, chosen by Him to bear witness to the Word. The Old Testament people of Israel is His instrument for the advent of Christ and the creation of a New Testament people who recognize Him as King and Son of God. They are a people led out of slavery through baptism into the freedom of faith, and are fed by Him on the way through the bread and wine of the sacrament. They are to testify of Him in all their dealings with their fellow men, but feel an especial attachment to those of the household of their faith. With them they come together to act as a people (leiturgia) before God, uniting with each other in prayer and praise and thanksgiving, in confession of sins and profession of faith, being built up in their common faith and life by the hearing of the Word and receiving of the sacrament.

It is in this context that we are to consider the sermon. It is not a form of discourse, autonomous in nature. Nor can it be explained by any rules of rhetoric. The sermon is embedded in the liturgy and derives its nature from the nature of the life of the congregation. A grave misunderstanding underlies the setting of the sermon over against the liturgy—a misunderstanding both of the liturgy and the sermon. Neither is "more important" than the other. They are parts of the one Word and complement each other. Liturgy holds the sermon to a Christ center; the sermon gives vitality to the worship of the congregation. In a good sense the liturgy is "form," giving form not only to the corporate worship but also giving "form" to the sermon.

For there is a relationship between the sermon and the elements of the liturgy which gives character to Lutheran preaching. It relates the sermon to the Word which is heard in lessons and seen in the sacrament. It binds preaching to the faith which the congregation professes in the Creed. It reflects the praise of the Gloria and the Hallelujah, the contrition of the Kyrie and Agnus Dei, the adoration of the Sanctus and Hosanna, the petitions of the collect and general prayer. It is the same Spirit that creates the faith of the congregation which uses the preacher to proclaim the Word. The same Word which bows the people to confession raises them to profession, and the Christ who is present in the sacrament is present in the Word that heals the sick of soul and gives courage to the weary.

A preacher who is not anchored to the liturgy may roam heaven and earth and the seas underneath for his "Topics." But his preaching is not organic to the people of God. It does not grow out of the soil, nor bear fruit on the vine. His sermons may be as beautiful as falling leaves or picked flowers, but they are thrown hither and thither by contemporary winds, or soon decay for want of relatedness to life. It is in the liturgical life of the people of God that the sermon grows out of the Word incarnate in human life.

3

The people of God find the meaning of time in the Church Year, and the scope of preaching is indicated by the Church Year and the lessons of the day.

The revelation of the Word comes in time, and the pattern of the message is seen in the various seasons of the church. The history of the Church Year traces an outline, beginning with Easter and Lent and Pentecost and going on to the observance of Epiphany and Christmas and Advent, and to the filling in of the year with the Epiphany and Trinity seasons and the days of the martyrs and the saints. Thus as on a wall of time is reflected the story of the eternal purpose of God's redemption.

But this, of course, is also the outline of the Scriptures, the fulfillment of an ancient promise and the eternal consequences of an historical event. God's creation of man, and His redemption of an erring humanity, are the message of a Word that has been spoken, has been recorded, but which is also the message of something still going on, a

Word that creates as it speaks, a Word that not only re-creates the past but creates a future.

As "deep calls to deep at the thunder of thy cataracts" (Ps. 42:7), so season speaks to season of the mercies of the Lord's year. The contents of the sermon are found in the message that Lent and Holy Week, Easter and Pentecost, Christmas and Trinity, bring annually before us. There is an order in God's revelation which becomes the master plan of Christian preaching. Preaching is not in vain for "Christ has been raised from the dead" and "in Christ shall all be made alive" (1 Cor. 15:20-22). The resurrection of the crucified Son of God and Son of man is the central theme of both the Church Year and the Christian sermon. From it flows all the richness and variety and power of Christian preaching. The crucifixion and resurrection lead the church to ask who He was and what God's purpose was in Him, what was the mind of Him who "humbled himself and became obedient unto death, even death on a cross," and on whom God has bestowed "the name which is above every name," before whom every knee should bow, in heaven and on earth and under the earth" (Phil. 2:5-11). It leads the church, also, to consider the consequences in the life of the individual, of human society, and of mankind. All the years are hardly enough to proclaim "the Lord's death, until He comes," His death, His resurrection, His return to judgment. The message is as broad as human life and it covers all of human time. The message inspires the congregation to praise and prayer. In the sacrament He is present who is the center of the service and of the year. In the sermon He speaks of the fullness which is God's revelation to man.

In this perspective we see the meaning of the pericopes, the lessons for the day. They suggest one small part of the whole message. They are not to be taken apart from the whole, for they derive their meaning from the Bible. But they focus for one day or week the subject of preaching on the particular aspect of the grace of God. They are one scene in the vast drama of redemption. Each lesson is one page in God's great book. As the congregation turns through the year following the motion of the Sun of righteousness, the Christian sermon heralds the message of the day and relates it to the eternal truth of the revelation of God.

4

The relating of preaching and the sacrament is as profound and comprehensive a matter as the fullness of faith itself. When either the sermon or the sacrament is subordinated to the other, something of the proper perspective of Christian truth is distorted. To say that the one is more fundamental or important than the other is to reveal a lack of appreciation of the one or the other. "Too much preaching" and "too much ritual" are both wide of the mark as an estimate of either sermon or liturgy.

How difficult the expression of the relationship is may be sensed from the architectural problem in the chancel construction. Is the attention of the congregation to be directed to the preacher? There are churches where the man in the pulpit is the center of attraction. There are denominations where "pulpit masters" are the criterion of the importance of the church. In the Lutheran Church, as a rule, the altar is supposed to be the central point toward which all else points. Here the administration of the sacrament is pre-eminent, and preaching may sometimes appear quite insignificant. It cannot be said that Lutheran church architecture has always solved the problem of the relationship satisfactorily. It has wavered between a medieval heritage of the centrality of the altar and a Reformed emphasis on the place of the pulpit. There is no typical Lutheran architecture which expresses the unique Lutheran conception of the balance between altar and pulpit. One wonders if the physical place of the sermon should not be the same as the spot where the lessons are read. For this would indicate the close bond between lessons and sermon, and give the sermon the connection with the rest of the liturgy which the lessons hold.

Another symptom of the uncertainty of the place of the sermon is the tendency to weave other elements of the liturgy around it as if it did not have an innate strength of position. I refer to the habit, ancient and modern, of introducing the sermon with prayer, or concluding with prayer. This reveals a lack of understanding of the meaning of the element of prayer in the other parts of the liturgy. Whatever can be said in the form of prayer in the pulpit can be said in those parts of the service where prayer is proper. To give the sermon its unique place we should let it stand forth as an independent or integral element. When the preacher goes to the pulpit he goes not to pray, not to give thanks, not to make announcements—he goes to proclaim the Word. We have weakened the effect of the sermon by all the extraneous and irrelevant items we have brought into the pulpit. The eccentricities of the preacher have no more place in the pulpit than at the altar.

There is a sense in which it might be held that the sermon is the key to liturgical worship. For if the sermon is man-centered, unrelated to the lessons of the Church Year, devoid of integration with the elements of the liturgy of which it is a part, then not only is the sermon "out of place," but the whole liturgy suffers, and the congregation has but gone to church to see a man perform. But if the sermon is carefully integrated with the prayer, the hymns, the lessons, the confession, the creed, even the benediction, and if it proclaims a Word somehow expressed or implicit in all the liturgy, then the worship has been an occasion for the Spirit of God to meet with the people and bind the hearts of all to himself.

5

The binding of the sermon to the Church Year and to the lessons of the liturgical worship is an expression of its relationship to the work of the Spirit in the congregation. Word and sacrament are directed to the edification of the people of God and are the means by which the Lord leads His people out of bondage toward the New Jerusalem. Christ is present in Word and sacrament to save from sin, and give power to walk in a new life. That life is characterized by penitence, confession, praise, prayer, adoration, love of neighbor and obedience to the will of God. The worship of the congregation and the proclamation of the Word are of the very essence of the community experience by which the people of God are called, gathered, enlightened and sanctified on earth, and preserved in union with Jesus Christ in the one true faith (Luther, Second Article).

Too often preaching of the Word is confused with an exegesis of the text of a portion of Scripture. While the Scriptures are the source of the sermon, the preacher is not engaged in a study of history, even sacred history, for its own sake. He is concerned about the story of God's dealing with His people, and all the marvelous events of their history is a revelation of the will and power of God to effect His purpose. As the psalmist and the prophets saw in the deliverance of Israel out of Egypt the evidence of God's liberation and preservation of a people of His own, so the New Testament preacher looks on all the mighty acts of the past as a revelation of Him who now is working to create a holy nation. The sermon continues that speaking of the Word which Jesus promised when He said, "I have yet many things to say to you, but you cannot hear them now. When the Spirit of truth comes, he will guide you into all the truth." (John 16:12, 13). The same Spirit that raised Christ from the dead dwells in the congregation into which we have been baptized so that in and through the Word which He proclaims "we too might walk in newness of life" (Rom. 6:4). The sermon is rooted in the past, because

God is He who worked in the past, but it moves into the present and future, for He is the same today and forever.

To His people Christ speaks both law and gospel. For the New Testament Israel is not, any more than the Old Testament Israel, ever a perfect people. There must be a daily dying unto sin, a constant repentance, as a result of the preaching. The people of the congregation must ever be sharpened in their sensitiveness to the will of God, so that they perceive wherein they fail in their love of God and love of neighbor. The sermon makes clear that until He comes, His body and His Word are given for us, and that we live continuously in the grace of His forgiveness. So the gospel is ever on the lips of the preacher. In the light of God's Word we see light for the daily task. In the abundance of God's mercy we receive the gift of dealing mercifully with our neighbor. Because God's love has been poured into our hearts through the Holy Spirit we have an unfailing hope (Romans 5:5).

The sermon is the bridge between the facts of the history of God's dealing with His people and the hope of a new life, a new earth and a new heaven, wherein we may find the goal of existence.

6

By the foregoing we do not deny that there may be preaching outside of the sanctuary and apart from a liturgical service. Actually, of course, the history of preaching includes the proclamation of the Word in places where no congregation exists, as in missionary endeavor, and at times when no liturgy expresses a congregational response. Even within the congregation there are so-called "preaching services" when the sermon is the main concern.

But always preaching presupposes a community of believers. The preacher comes out of such a community. His message is from the household of faith. And the goal of preaching is to form a congregation where none exists, to build up a community where there was none. Where the congregation is present the sermon seeks to perfect that which has been begun. All preaching may, therefore, be termed congregational in its character.

This is not a restriction on preaching. Rather it is a widening of the meaning of the congregation. It is through the congregation that Word and sacrament build a people which is God's instrument for the redemption of the world. There is much preaching that conceives of the congregation as a closed body of congenial spirits who presume to be the body of Christ. But man may not define the limits of the people of God and claim that any distinct group is identifiable with the Church of Christ. Yet within the world is a people known to God which receives and transmits the message of the Word. It is a creative Word, and the reacting congregation responds to the Word in the prayer and praise of the liturgy, in the hearing of the Word and in the reception of the sacrament. Out of this community comes a knowledge of the will of God for all people, for the nation and the individual, for all of life, whatever be the vocation or occupation. The congregation is the image of the people of God on earth, and through it mankind is prepared for the heavenly worship which is life with God.

The sermon is an inalienable part of the Word and sacrament and participates in the action whereby men are buried with Christ in baptism so as to become members of the new body of humanity of which Christ is head. The sermon may be little more than the reading of the lessons in the liturgy or it may be a highly developed form of making known the Word. In either case it is a means whereby the Spirit of God bears and fosters children in the household of God. The words of institution in the Lord's Supper are themselves a proclamation of the Word, and the Word is itself sacramental, so that Word and sacrament may not be pitted against each other or thought of as mutually exclusive. The Word is proclaimed too in all the sacramental acts whereby the church seeks to bring all of life's great experiences under the heaven of the Word.

The goal, both of the sermon and all the liturgy, is nothing less than the redemption of the world. To principalities and powers in the heavenly places the manifold wisdom of God and the unsearchable riches of Christ are to be made known, by word and worship and witness "to make all men see what is the plan of the mystery hidden for ages in God who created all things."

The Meaning and Task of the Sermon in the Framework of the Liturgy

By Bishop Bo Giertz

1.

No liturgy without a sermon. This basic principle has remained for us evangelicals since the Reformation. It is faithfully observed by all Lutheran churches in the world. Where a divine service is held without a sermon, it may immediately be said that we are dealing with a "special" service. It goes without saying that it is not unevangelical to order prayer devotions, intercessions, and daily, short divine services, and the like, with only liturgy and without a sermon. It is, however, just as self-evident to us that such divine services could not replace the main divine service of Sunday. And at the main service there is always preaching. In an emergency—for example, in the remote villages of Northern Sweden—when a lay service is conducted and some pious farmer reads the liturgy of the "high mass" (a practice increasingly rare in our modern age of radio), then he also reads a sermon aloud. Without a sermon it would not be a proper divine service. And when Holy Communion is held outside the high mass in early mornings, evenings, or workdays (a practice that has been rising rapidly in Sweden during the last twenty years), then the agenda calls for a meditation on confession to be given which is equivalent to a sermon. These conditions are not far different from those in other Lutheran churches.

Is it merely chance or historical circumstance that this situation exists among us today? Or, instead, do there still stand facts behind this principle which are as binding today as they were four hundred years ago? What is the relation of the sermon to the liturgy?

To answer this question, we must briefly address ourselves first to the meaning and task of the liturgy.

2.

The meaning and task of the liturgy is to render possible the communal relation between the congregation and God. Liturgy is an expression of life from the body of Christ. As the body of Christ, the congregation should assemble and go before God as a unity, as a "corporate body" in its true sense, in order to receive His gifts and, from His side, to bring forth the spiritual sacrifice of the new covenant. In thanks and praise, in confession of sin and intercession, in the reception of Word and sacrament, in all these the church practices the priestly service to which the believers as a royal people of priests are called.

The liturgy is therefore necessary. Where the liturgical life of the church is stunted, the new life in Christ cannot develop in its full riches. Where the divine service is limited to the sermon, supplemented only by a few sung hymns and a free prayer by the pastor, there something essential has been lost. The general prayer, the praise of the whole congregation, the imploring Kyrie uniting all voices into one, the cultic rejoicing as it comes to expression in the Gloria, the Sanctus, and the Benedictus—the church can dispense with none of these. In the liturgy the most important experiences of faith are represented again and again. The Christian participates therein not as a pious private person, but as a member of the mystical body of Christ. Liturgy is eternal. In heaven the confession of sin ceases. The Kyrie becomes silent and the Agnus Dei transforms itself into the praise of the Lamb who has purchased us with His blood. But the whole heaven is filled with one exuberant Gloria, Hallelujah, and Benedicamus.

Difficulties with the liturgy are well known to us all. Religious individualism rears itself against the impulse to adapt one's pious feelings to the congregation and to come before God in the uniformity of the agenda. Here the church must constantly admonish, "He who cannot love his brother whom he can see, how can he love God whom he cannot see?" If we are truly one in Christ, we must also be able to pray and praise together.

On the other hand, it is thoroughly understandable when beginners, or those strange to the life of the church, assert that they receive nothing from the liturgy and that they come to church only because of the sermon. That is how it must be at the beginning. It is naturally hard for those who are not firmly attached to the body of Christ to join in the priestly service of that body. Here one can only quietly say, "Wait, it will all come before long. Be observant, familiarize yourself, let the Word speak, let it work, and you will also understand the rest."

3.

The meaning of the sermon is not to bring the priestly office of the believers into realization. The sermon, rather, exercises the prophetic office of Christ. Preaching comes through the Word of Christ, and for that reason brings forth faith.

The Word works and creates faith. The sermon addresses itself also to those estranged from the church. A proper sermon has also something to say to them. It holds a mirror before our eyes in which we can come to know ourselves as we really look, as we really appear in the eyes of God. It paints for us the picture of the Savior. It shows His presence among us. His voice resounds again in the world; He makes His way through the crowds; His powerful deeds occur once again. The eyes of the blind are opened, and to the poor is proclaimed the joyful message of the forgiveness of sins. The sermon also maintains this purpose and these tasks over against the believers. Faith is always worked anew. It is a life process which may never cease in this age. The law reveals the sin; the gospel heals the wounds. Indeed there is a progression in the sermon. One gives only milk to the young children in Christ. To the mature one may speak wisdom. Yet the task of the sermon remains fundamentally the same: ✳ to create faith, to make Christ contemporary, to build the church.

In heaven, therefore, the sermon ceases. There faith belongs to the very being of the new humanity. It is no longer endangered by Satan and the Old Adam. The liturgy, however, sounds forth eternally.

4.

The relation between sermon and liturgy can now be described. The sermon is fundamental. Without preaching there is no faith. The sermon creates the new life in Christ, it incorporates us into the body of Christ, and continually leads its members to this life. (I am consciously disregarding the sacraments here, which do the same thing.) This new life, then, unfolds itself in the liturgy, just as it does in love to our neighbors, in one's calling, and in many other ways which are not under consideration here.

Without preaching there can be no proper liturgy. To be sure, where the gospel is rightly preached one can very well conduct a divine service now and then without a sermon. For long duration, however, no congregation can live without a sermon. It could if faith were merely a *fides historica,* a knowledge of the Triune God which one could acquire once for all. Faith on earth, however, is never a property which cannot be lost. It is a manner of life which is constantly being re-created by God, as the Word continually works repentance and leads us to the Savior. Faith can only live in daily repentance and conversion. A living liturgy, in which we worship God in spirit and in truth, can only come into being where the living Word is at work.

5.

The sermon and the liturgy bear a mutual influence upon each other. The position of the sermon in the church will be conditioned by the position of the liturgy and the interpretations placed upon it. On the other hand, a proper sermon also exercises a certain influence upon the liturgy. We will come back to this point later, but first very briefly—and in all too summary a fashion—we shall demonstrate how a false relationship can be established.

The Roman depreciation of the sermon is clearly connected with the Roman teachings on the sacraments, faith, and the liturgy as a meritorious work. Where the sacraments work *ex opere operato,* where the proper faith is an essential acknowledgment of the teaching of the church, and where participation in the liturgy—with exception of the state of mortal sin—is always considered a *meritum,* there it is self-evident that one cannot grant the place for the sermon which it just as self-evidently must have with us. In the Roman Church the liturgy lives its own life. It cannot experience any influence from the sermon. It does not even need to employ the language of the people.

Much of the same could be said of the Anglicans. It is always strange for a Swede to hear what incidental and superficial themes can be treated in the short addresses of the Anglican divine services. They often appear to stand in no inner connection with the Mass being celebrated. I always think that here one can most clearly detect how little some Anglicans understand of the *articulus justificationis*. A pious lady from the Episcopal Church in the United States once told me after a Lutheran sermon which she had accidentally heard, "How powerful that was, so very different from ours. It was as if a message had come to us directly from God."

Here also the liturgy lives its own life. Since it is a liturgy in the vernacular with Biblical readings strongly represented, the situation is far more favorable than in the Roman Church. Yet a Lutheran will always miss something essential. He will often envy the beauty of the Anglican liturgy. We would all like to have more of the activity of the laity, the lively antiphonal singing, and the well-composed prayers which so ably unite the dignified with the fervent. Since the sermon is attached so loosely, often as a kind of accidental address or communication of the pastor, and since sin and grace are not fundamental in the preaching, the liturgy always runs the danger of being understood as the Old Man in us always understands it: as a good and meritorious work which makes us into Christians. In this way, on Anglican soil, one can so closely approach Rome that finally only some external questions, such as, primacy, the marriage of priests, and the like, remain as dividing factors.

6.

How does this reciprocal action between sermon and liturgy take place among us?

a) The sermon works the life which the liturgical forms must fill out. Where the conscience is awakened by the sermon, the confession of sin becomes a serious matter and the Kyrie sounds with a new fervency. Where the Holy Spirit absolves the conscience through the Word, there one can sing His Gloria with new joy. An awakening usually also means a renewal of worship life and congregational singing. There are exceptions. In nineteenth century Sweden, we experienced a far-reaching revival—the so-called "New Evangelism"—in which thousands of our church members were alienated from every liturgy. The causes were dissimilar. A strong Reformed influence contributed to it. The Lutheran divine service was more than once so diluted and spiritless through rationalism and secularism that it was rejected as empty formalism.

However, where living preaching takes place in a living church, and where this preaching brings forth fruits, there one may reckon that liturgy will also be invigorated anew.

b) Liturgy gives the sermon its framework, its preparation, and its recession. It provides the stillness, the turning toward God. It also gives the theme for the day. It gives the plan for the Church Year which the proclamation has to follow. It hinders the preacher from limiting himself merely to his own favorite texts. It works so that the congregation may, as far as possible, be offered the whole Biblical message. In these ways the sermon is decisively influenced by the liturgy. The structure of the Church Year and the selection of the pericopes determine the sermon. One has only to think what it has meant to Swedish homiletics that we have always celebrated the Purification and Annunciation of Mary, St. John's Day, St. Michael's Day, and All Saints' Day.

7.

How must the sermon be formed in order to fulfill its meaning and task in the framework of the liturgy?

First, it must not be especially "liturgical." It must not in any special way become liturgically constructed. Many pastors have a dangerous inclination to do this. The sermon is introduced by a special small liturgy which includes an apostolic greeting, hymn reading, set prayers, the Trinitarian formula and other things. Such a fixed introduction to the sermon is often only a meaningless duplication of the liturgy already celebrated. The greeting was already there (in the *Salutatio*), as was the appropriate prayer (in the *Collecta*); and the sermon hymn should have completed the essential preparation of prayer. Personally, I am of the opinion that sermon preambles in the pulpit should be as short as possible. A brief prayer, usually a free one, will in most cases be sufficient.

The pastor must further guard himself against employing a liturgically colored sermon language. Liturgical language is polished for universal validity. It consciously avoids the concrete and the special. It should condense as much as possible and express it in general terms. Totally different is the sermon: it must try to address a concrete individual directly in his special situation. The liturgy speaks quite generally about sin, and must do so. The sermon must aim precisely at individual sins. The sermon is not stylized, not condensed generalities. It is concrete, actual, boldly realistic. It is liturgically proper to form one's sermon in such a way that whatsoever the liturgy presents in its timeless and elevated style is translated into as everyday and modern and truthful a manner as possible.

Secondly, the connection of the sermon to the liturgy should not consist in its providing liturgical instruction. To be sure, one must often explain the liturgy, and not only for confirmands. It can often be very fitting to insert some little liturgical instruction in the sermon. But it may not be practiced in such a manner that the sermon becomes an exposition of liturgy. The sermon should also not begin with some notes on the history of liturgy in regard to the background of the theme for the day. The attention of the congregation, however, should be directed to the theme of the day. This takes place when the theme is presented as *God's* message for the day. It may be somewhat in this form: "God will show us today in his Word how . . . We heard it already in the Epistle, Gospel, etc. . . ." We should not begin: "The text for this day was chosen more than a thousand years ago as the Lombards grievously threatened the church and the people in Italy . . ." In the divine service we are not carrying on liturgical instruction. We are celebrating a holy liturgy and proclaiming glad tidings.

Thirdly, in the interest of liturgy, we must demand that the sermon be truly *prophetic*. It should proclaim the Word as *God's* Word. One must ever and again perceive: Thus speaks the Lord. The sermon has an *opus divinum* to direct. It must proclaim the law to the unrepentant and confirm the death sentence of the Old Man. It should bar the way of evasion, silence the mouth of self-righteousness, and bring grace to the weary and the burdened. This may seem self-evident. Nevertheless, it is unfortunately not so in practice. It ought to be so according to the principles of our church as based upon the Lutheran understanding of Holy Scripture. Yet in most Lutheran churches another kind of preaching is more frequently to be heard. It is the apologetic or "presbyter-centered" sermon where the pastor is the subject who expounds his opinions, his learning, and his experiences. Or there is the sermon which has many good things to say about Christianity, Christian views, and the Christian life, but never gets around to saying, "This is it. Thus saith the Lord. Repent and have faith in the gospel!"

A sermon which does not proclaim the law and the gospel in the name of God is an unliturgical sermon. The liturgy presupposes the presence of God as self-evident. We are gathered together to worship

Him and hear His voice. Anyone who suddenly begins to speak *about* God as if he were a far-distant phenomenon whose deeds and wishes were an object of ambiguous reflection, is completely out of style. A sermon, however, which proclaims God's Word in His name has properly understood its place within the liturgy even if it is completely lacking in style.

The liturgical framework, then, is not without meaning for such a prophetic sermon. First, from the very beginning, the liturgy says that the Lord is in His holy temple. It places the congregation before God. Secondly, as said, the liturgy provides us with our theme. Every pastor who is bound to fixed pericopes knows what a blessing it is. It is of the spirit of the religious "enthusiasts" to believe that a prophetic sermon—in the sense developed above—necessitates a free selection of texts. It pleased God to work through the Word. The church carries this Word through all the centuries to all peoples. Through its pericopes the church ascertains what it considers as indispensable. This is the minimum which must be preached to every congregation. And since God speaks in His Word, it must be possible every Sunday to interpret even the prescribed text in such a way that the Lord speaks here again.

This is, then, the task of the sermon within the framework of the liturgy: to preach the given Word so that the God who is present can speak to His children and reveal His will to them. When this happens, then God also creates the repentance, the faith, and the new life which, in turn, find their own self-expression within the liturgy.

8.

If the sermon fails, then the liturgy can step in for the sermon as an expedient under certain circumstances. This must be said to supplement what has been said above. If the Word of God does not come to expression in the sermon, then the word of the liturgy, the nearness of God in the sacraments, and the dogma of the church hymns will often compensate for the absence of the sermon. It is common knowledge that God can also create a living faith where bad preaching is heard. Yet that does not prove that we have overestimated the sermon. It is always a state of emergency in the church if the message of the Son of God, the only Redeemer, is proclaimed mainly through the church's liturgy and hymns. It appears also that church life is best renewed by the strength of able sermons. Unfortunately it is true, however, that not seldom has the liturgy remained the true proclaimer of the gospel. When the liturgy was stunted and strongly cut, as in the days of liberal theology, the results were worse than usual. One could ask whether the relatively active congregational life in England is not connected with the richness of its liturgy. Despite the mediocre sermons, the Word and the doctrine lived in the congregation. In many Lutheran congregations during the liberal age of the Enlightenment the Word was condemned to a much greater extent to silence.

If we find in Sweden today a strong trend toward liturgy, hourly prayers, and frequent communion, we must accept this as a serious sign of our homiletical weakness. This trend, in and of itself, is good and should be encouraged. But it is also the fruit of an emergency situation. Our laity tell us candidly that the sermon has too little to offer them. They experience much more of God's power and goodness when they sing their hymns, read their Psalter, or participate in the liturgy, and commune. One cannot forbid them this. Yet we preachers should seriously ask ourselves what we have made of the living Word, if it has so little to say to our people. This question is addressed to theology, to the exegetes and systematicians, to the church leaders and the whole clergy. The church of the Word cannot afford a good conscience until the sermon has once again found its meaning and task within the framework of the liturgy.

The Confessional and the Communion Service

By Prof. Christhard Mahrenholz

I. *Admission to Holy Communion*

1. As God's GIFTS OF GRACE, both Word and sacrament bring the living and incarnate Son of God, Jesus Christ. At the same time, the church, which has been entrusted with the administration of these gifts of grace, dares not overlook the differences between the Word and sacrament which are inherent in their nature and in the manner of their offering. To do so is to invite serious trouble. One of the essential differences consists in the following: The read or preached Word is addressed fundamentally to and for the general public, so that everyone can hear it. It is within the very commission of the church itself that the Word is to go out beyond the walls of the "church," in order to exert as great a sphere of influence as possible. The Sacrament of the Altar, on the other hand, is administered only in the narrower sphere of the Christian congregation. It is meant exclusively for the baptized, and even for these there are restrictions and limitations. Such limitations in the admission to Holy Communion —as over against the unlimited admission to the sermon—have a threefold cause.

(a)   According to the Apostle Paul (1 Cor. 11:27, 29), one takes upon oneself a heavy guilt if one receives the sacrament *"anaxiōs"* (adverbial: in an unworthy manner; not adjectival: as one unworthy). He is guilty of the body and blood of the Lord, and sins against the holy, thereby taking the sacrament in "damnation to himself." Herein lie the roots for sacramental discipline in the Christian Church and for the fact that, from the very beginning, the office of the liturgist—who administered the sacrament—was bound up together with the office of the congregational leader, who decided over the "discipline." Public sinners, who were not disposed to repentance but persisted in their sin, were thereby excluded from participation in the sacrament. This was not carried out merely for the sake of a temporal congregational or disciplinary order, or even because of the warranted offense which had been caused to the congregation. Far more was the sacramental fellowship broken off in order to protect the sinner against the gravest danger of receiving the body and blood of the Lord to his own damnation. The Lutheran Reformation obstinately held fast to the fact that sacramental participation is a "dangerous" enterprise, which can lead to a damnation instead of a blessing. This is the so-called "little ban": the only occasion given the spiritual office for removing one of the baptized from the number of those entitled to the sacrament.

(b)   Luther saw much deeper into the meaning of "unworthy" than had the church before him.

The transition in the meaning of unworthy which had commenced already in the early church resulted in an interpretation of moral merit. Luther repudiated a *moral* interpretation of the concepts "worthy" and "unworthy," as if they could be measured on a scale of differently weighted sins. He understood the notion "worthy" once again in its proper adverbial sense (e.g. Small Catechism: "Who, then, receives such a sacrament worthily?"). Ultimately, for Luther, the worthy reception of the sacrament is conditioned by faith in the words "for you" in the sacrament's institution. Faith and unbelief are determined for Luther through the categories "gospel" and "law." He who receives the sacrament in the faith that through the death and resurrection of Christ his justification is worked *sola fide,* receives it under the impression of the gospel; i.e., to him is dedicated, as a gift of salvation, the broken body and shed blood of Jesus Christ. He who receives the sacrament in unbelief, however, receives it under the impression of the law; i.e., he eats only the body of Christ and drinks His blood, without its being dedicated to him as a gift of salvation.

[144]

Thereby he becomes jointly responsible for the crucifixion of the Lord and incurs death. When the definitions of "worthy" and "unworthy" are identical with those of "faith" and "unbelief" in this sense, then moral categories are clearly excluded.

When this faith is determinative, moreover, then its external pre-conditions must be given: The Christian must have knowledge and understanding of the sacrament in order that he might properly distinguish the body of Christ from the natural, non-sacramental foods, as well as from false sacraments. Prior to the Reformation, the church understood this distinction in a relatively external fashion and usually tied it together with the child's use of reason at about the age of 10. The Reformation demanded a lot more. It turned away from such a *rational* interpretation of the notion "worthy" and sought far more, by way of the *Catechism,* to develop and strengthen "true faith." Herein lies the starting point for the Reformation's recreation of "confirmation," a practice which was originally repeated annually by all Christians, but which later became limited to a onetime act expressing one's right of admission to the sacrament. This admission was dependent upon a catechetical examination,[1] and upon a public testimony of faith in the act of confirmation. Therefore, in the Lutheran church, confirmation and admission to Holy Communion are not to be separated.

There is, to be sure, a pedagogical interpretation of the idea "worthy" which proceeds from the viewpoint that Luther's demand for faith in Part V of the Catechism is to be understood solely in terms of the result of churchly training in doctrine. Over against this view, it must be maintained that confirmation is not only catechetical interrogation, but also an action of intercession and blessing: The congregation in communal prayer and the office-holder in personal words of "special comfort" pray that the confirmands might remain in true faith, which is itself the sole precondition for worthy reception. Among the efforts in the early Lutheran Church pointing toward this proper understanding of the sacrament was the new form of the confession (Cf. sec. 6 below).

(c) The discipline described above (a) applies only for public sinners who demand to take the sacrament frivolously. Here the church must intervene in order that the holy might not be given to "dogs" (the unrepentant), and the sinners not partake with harm to body and soul. And yet it does not say in 1 Cor. 11:28, "Let the bishop examine every communicant and then admit him," but rather, "Let a man examine himself." Where no open sins are involved, so that the congregation need not intervene for the protection of the holiness of the sacraments, the responsibility always and in every case remains with the baptized. This neither can nor may be taken from him. Understandable only in this context is the sentence: *De occultis non judicat ecclesia.* To be sure, the church, in its ordinance, should not frivolously support a false practice of the freedom which belongs to each single baptized member. Along with the early church, we also demand that the Christian go forward from his place to the altar, testifying by his rising and going to his own personal decision. We refuse to carry the sacrament to the communicant's place in the nave, for the danger then prevails that one partake of the sacrament against one's will, in order "not to give offense." Nor may the church (for the same reason) support any movement whereby the congregation is led to the altar pew by pew by the sacristan. It must be avoided that anyone is simply "taken up along with the rest" to receive the sacrament.

2.   If one examines this threefold protective ring which the church has placed around the Sacrament of the Altar on the basis of Holy Scripture, one comes to the conclusion that while (1b) is somewhat practiced, and (1c) is at least recognized in principle, yet (1a) is almost completely unobserved, since it is possible only in some few small congregations and virtually impossible in most city congregations. Herein lies a heavy loss for our church life. The church must face the question whether it must not partition its congregations that are too large, not because it is sociologically or organizationally expedient, but because it is basically *necessary* for the proper administration of the sacrament.

3.   Now it is universally the practice in church order, however, to make admission to Holy Communion dependent upon a previous confession. This uniting of confession and Holy Communion is considered so self-evident that in some of our liturgies the two stand together under a single rubric! From this viewpoint, the ordinance to celebrate the sacrament within the main service is characterized as questionable, for then members of the congregation can also partake of Holy Communion who have not already been to confession. While the equation of the confessing and communing congregations is taken for granted as self-evident, the difference between the worshiping and communing congregations is stressed. From similar considerations, it is demanded that the main divine service contain within itself a regular confessional with both confession of sin and absolution, for only in this way can the proper preparation of the communicants be in-

sured. Now it is uncontested that Scripture nowhere demands a connection of confession and Holy Communion (Cf. the presentation of Peter Brunner in *Leiturgia*), and that the confession does not belong to the threefold protective ring around the Sacrament of the Altar (Cf. sec. 2 above). Yet it still remains to be clarified whether the connection between confession and Holy Communion is not useful on practical grounds, or whether the traditional practice of coupling the two does not in fact contain so many weaknesses that it would appear advisable for the church to revise its practice.

II. *The Confession*

4. Along with Luther and his doctrine of confession, we understand and use "confession" here as comprising both the confession of sin *and* its absolution as necessary elements. A confessional prayer of the pastor without the "yes" of the penitent and without the assurance of forgiveness is not "confession" as understood here, but rather "confession of sin" (*confiteor* or public guilt). On the relation of these elements to the main divine service, see the *Agende*, I, 3, p. 15ff. and I, 4, p. 40. (Order of Service for Lutheran churches and congregations.)

5. Originally, the confession had no connection with the celebration of Holy Communion in the Christian Church. The members of the congregation went regularly every Sunday to the Table of the Lord without any special churchly or religious preparation seen as necessary. Grounds for exclusion were limited to childhood (1b), open sin (1a), or self-exclusion (1c). The reception of the sacrament took on the character of a regular occurrence (". . . this do in remembrance of me") in the same fashion as the hearing of the Word and the holding of a regular service in general. The confession, however, from the very outset, was a *casus,* a special case having to do with some depressed and frightened Christian who had lapsed into sin or suffered pangs of conscience and guilt. We know that for a long time the church shrank from using the full power of the Lord in the handling of the binding and loosing keys as is our common practice today, but preferred rather to say a prayer of intercession for the forgiveness of sins over the contrite. We also know that on the basis of the New Testament words of institution of the office of the keys, the church was led further here in its pastoral care and declared the forgiveness *expressis verbis* to individuals in the power of the Lord. We know further how Martin Luther also maintained confession and absolution as a special form for the individual's confession of his shortcomings and reception of the pardoning Word of God. For reasons which we

cannot fully develop here (e.g., the theological interpretation of the concept "mortal sin" and the practice of "Easter duty"), it is clear that already in the pre-Reformation church, the confession had come into a relation with Holy Communion at least to the extent that the duty to commune at Easter was made dependent upon a prior confession. But it is of importance that Luther maintained the *casus* character of confession, the character of dependence upon special causes and circumstances, of a voluntary rather than a compulsory nature. He repudiated any forced confession while supporting and maintaining the pre-Reformation church practice of a regulated and regular reception of the sacrament. Already, then, on this basis Luther could not demand a fixed coupling of confession and Holy Communion, for it would involve the uniting of two disparate elements whose fundamental practices (regular vs. occasional according to requirement or necessity) could not be joined together.[2]

6. Yet Luther never transferred this fundamental separation into the practice of a set relationship. In the main, he employed the pre-Reformation practice of making the reception of the sacrament dependent upon a prior confession in order to instruct the unknowing members of the congregation in the knowledge and understanding of the Christian faith (Cf. sec. 1b above). In other words, he used it to supplement their faulty catechetical instruction. Under the heading of "confessional examination," therefore, we often find a regulated and well-founded catechetical examination, geared to meet prevailing needs. No one will deny that this emergency institution at the outset of the Reformation was a great blessing. It guarded against the misuse and dishonoring of the sacrament by congregations which often communed only by virtue of accepted custom, without knowing what was being given to them in the sacrament. And yet, it is just as indisputable that the designation of the catechetical examination as "confession" is basically a misunderstanding. The rule in many of the seventeenth century church ordinances that one must first have gone to confession before receiving holy communion is perhaps tenable as long as one understands thereby the catechetical interrogation, but certainly can no longer be accepted if one is thinking of a proper confession with both confession of sin and absolution. As the development then moved from private confession to congregational confession, it usually led to a severing of the celebration of Holy Communion from the main service with the confession being tacked on. This meant that it was no longer possible either to confess or to commune separately. As a total misconception of Luther's fundamental intentions,

this practice worked to the disadvantage of both confession and Holy Communion, especially since it was no longer possible to realize and to experience both acts in divine service in the uniqueness of their peculiar gifts, concerns, and preconditions.

7. In the moment when private confession is again considered of beneficial value, as has been the case in the Lutheran Church, then the formerly established unity of corporate confession and the celebration of Holy Communion is no longer tenable. He who has gone to private confession no longer partakes in the corporate confession, and thereby is lost the previously prevailing identity of the confessing and communing congregations which alone could justify the liturgical coupling of confession and Holy Communion. Then both elements are once again directed to themselves and their own peculiar forms and gifts.

8. Just as little can the incorporation of Holy Communion into the main service have the consequence that in every main service a proper confession with absolution also be held. This is not only because the main service would thereby be overloaded, if one had the confession as well as the sermon and Holy Communion. It is also because the confession— even the so-called "public confession"— is fundamentally a non-public action in which those unite who desire individually to give their "Yes" to the confession of sin and receive the individual absolution of their sin. It is questionable to undertake such an act before a gathering of non-participants. It is even more doubtful to lead such a gathering as a whole into a confession of sin and then to declare absolution to them, when there are some members of the congregation present who are unwilling either to confess or to be absolved at that time. (See *Agende* 1, 3, 15ff. where it is clearly emphasized that the matters at hand are different in the *confiteor* and the open guilt, for there we deal with a general confessional and not with a formal absolution.

III. *The Relation of Confession to Holy Communion*

9. With a fundamental separation of confession and Holy Communion, each could be restored to its peculiar function. Confession— either private or corporate—could be liberated from its fixation with Holy Communion. Contrariwise, the incorporation of Holy Communion into the service could no longer be rejected on the ground that no confession had taken place in or before the service. It is of the greatest importance that confession be restored to its independent role, and not used merely as the door for Holy Communion.

10. The responsibility entrusted to the church by Scripture to help its members in their self-examination (Cf. sec. 1c above) is not met merely by incorporating confessional questions and absolution into the main service, or by offering the *confiteor* and the open guilt as substitutes. It is a basic error and evasion of the real decision to think that one has done enough to comply with the demands of Scripture for protecting the sacrament against unworthy reception by inserting prayer, questions, answers, and absolution of a confessional as a kind of purifying filter before the reception of Holy Communion. For this approach lays the accent upon the "objective" side of the matter with its dangerous mortgage of the menacing mechanistic practice of loaded conveyances of grace. Stressed here is the objectivity of the forgiveness of sins which is mediated through the absolution which is given again, in any case, in the sacrament itself. But it is the "personal" side which should here be stressed: the impulse for self-examination, the clarifying of our unworthiness, the sharpening of the conscience, the pointing toward faith which clings to the saving gift of God. In *Agende* I, that which is decisive is far better expressed by the optional offering of the invitation for preparation *(confiteor)* than by the formal confession with absolution (Cf. also *Agende* I, 4, p. 39ff.).

11. Once this fundamental clarity has been won concerning a separately held confession—whether private or corporate— we see that along with many other possibilities, this practice would also provide a real service to the proper preparation for Holy Communion by offering the occasion for confessional counsel, the opening of the heart through the preached Word, and the direct address with the penitent in a small circle rather than in the presence of the whole congregation. Therefore, once confession and Holy Communion have been fundamentally separated, the congregation should be offered and constantly reminded of the opportunity for confession before, or at least near, every celebration of Holy Communion, especially there where the custom already prevails. As a rule, such confession would usually be corporate; i.e., the simultaneous confession of many. It dare not be overlooked that the preparation for Holy Communion is also a *casus* which can give impulse for confession. Here a whole group of congregational members have the same *casus* for confession which, in this case, is publicly known and intelligible. Moreover, when the personal situation or life conduct of a Christian calls for private confession (the celebration of which as *private* is clearly fitting in these circumstances), then the common confession also has its good purpose when

the *casus* consists in corporate participation in Holy Communion. The proper self-examination of the communicants can also be demanded in the confessional exhortation, thereby meeting the concern which early Lutheranism expressed—though with a relevant accentuation on the pedagogical—with the term "catechetical examination."

12. The publicly known and unrepentant sinners who are excluded from the church's sacramental fellowship will be readmitted to the sacrament, once they are contrite and seek forgiveness (loosening of the small ban). This admission occurs in the confession: through the declaration of absolution, the communal fellowship is once again restored. In this case, the confession is necessary prior to the return to communal fellowship by the repentant sinner. The form, however (private or corporate), is optional.

13. With the exception of this case (under 12), there may never be made any demand for participation in confession, or for the establishing of confession as a prerequisite for reception of the sacrament. On the contrary, the opportunity for confession must be given unconnected with the Holy Communion, and the congregation should be encouraged in its practice.

14. In conclusion: Holy Scripture obligates the church which has restored the Sacrament of the Altar to the service

    (a)   to practice sacramental discipline in regard to open sinners (1a) earnestly and fearlessly, and

    (b)   to help secret sinners in their self examination prior to the reception of Holy Communion.

One such important and essential help to (b) is the confession, especially in its conversation and exhortation. But the confession is neither the only nor the indispensable means to advise in each specific situation. This affirmation means neither a depreciation nor a devaluation of the confession, but on the contrary, is a recognition of the special function and great importance which the confession has, once it is liberated from any false unity with the Sacrament, in the life of the Christian congregation, especially here in regard to the worthy reception of the Sacrament of the Altar.

NOTES

[1] It is these catechetical examinations which the Lutheran Confessions have in mind when they say that no one "unexamined" should be permitted to Holy Communion. Today, we would say "unconfirmed."

[2] In the light of this *fundamental* assertion, it should not be overlooked that, while Luther also repudiated any forced confession even at Easter, it is still greatly to be desired that good confessional practice also express itself in a certain regularity. The fundamentally different estimates of the Sacrament and the confession are not given up, however, even when the casual character of confession and the fixed character of sacramental reception are limited in actual church practice.

Worship and Sacrifice

By Rector Carl Fr. Wislöff

OUR THEME TOUCHES a point of interconfessional controversy. Apart from monasticism as the foundation on which the papacy was built, Luther saw its greatest "abomination" in the sacrifice of the mass. In the history of Lutheranism, to be sure, this question concerning the idea of sacrifice in worship has hardly been touched for a long time. If now the question of the Lord's Supper and sacrifice is opening up again in many places, and is becoming the object of a thoroughgoing investigation within evangelical Christendom also, it would appear absolutely necessary to handle the question from the way it was decisively put during the Reformation period itself. If we do not do this, we will run the danger of withdrawing from the problems presented by conversation with the Catholic Church.

From this point of view the question of worship and sacrifice becomes, primarily, a question of the relationship of the Lord's Supper and sacrifice. Just here was where the *status controversiae* of the Reformation period lay, and where the chief problem of our own time lies as well.

First we wish to present briefly Luther's objections to the sacrifice of the mass. In *De captivitate babylonica* and in his *Treatise on the New Testament* Luther takes exception to two things: First, the mass has been made into a "work"; and second, the sacrament has been made into a "sacrifice." These are two quite different viewpoints which overflow into each other in presentation, but which can very well be viewed separately.

The first—the mass as a work— has to do with the piety of the mass. Whereas the Lord's Supper, according to the words of institution, is purely a gift of God, the mass had been turned into a kind of performance on the part of man. Here, where God himself sets the table and everything is so completely prepared that, on our part, nothing else is asked than a thirsty soul, humility, and readiness to receive, men now began, instead, to busy themselves with their own preparation, their own worthiness before God and their own expressions of piety. The mass was simply made to serve that work-righteousness which is the religion of the natural man.

The result is either despair or else the false security which is, in fact, its immediate neighbor. In both instances this work-righteousness means an abrogation of the completed work of Christ on the cross. If we make the mass into a work, we scorn that blood shed for the sake of grace. The mass is, therefore, a constant re-crucifixion of Jesus Christ, and that is also true of pilgrimages, alms, and the other self-chosen deeds of self-centered piety.

We should like to linger at this point a moment. Seen historically, this objection is really the only one that continued to be raised to the sacrifice of the mass. This is already apparent in Melanchthon's *Apology to the Augsburg Confession*, Art. XXIV of which is to examine: *quid sit sacrificium, et quae sint sacrificii species* [what a sacrifice is, and what the kinds of sacrifice are]. It is characteristic of his whole treatment that Melanchthon begins with the concept of "ceremonia oder heilig Werk" [ceremony, or a sacred action or work]. His interest is in the liturgical action and his question ultimately is this: What should a Christian think of the action in the Lord's Supper? This determines his whole treatment of the subject. *Ceremonia* is the overall concept under which he includes two others: The first is *sacramentum—in quo Deus nobis exhibet hoc, quod offert annexa ceremoniae promissio* [sacrament—in which God gives to us that which the promise connected with the ceremony offers]. The essential thing in the Sacrament is, therefore, that God grants something to us through it. As an example he can mention baptism which is a ceremony or work which we do not present to God, but through which God gives us the forgiveness of sins according to His promise. The second concept is *sacrificium—quod nos Deo reddimus, ut eum honore afficiamus* [sacrifice—that which we render God in order to bestow Him with honor]. Sacrifice is an action directed toward God, a human action to His glory.

Furthermore, Melanchthon explains that there are two kinds of sacrifice: sacrifice of propitiation and sacrifice of thanksgiving. In order to show that, rightly understood, the Lord's Supper also has the character of a sacrifice, Melanchthon uses a method of logical reduction. The Eucharist cannot be a sacrifice of propitiation for there is only one sacrifice of propitiation in the New Covenant, namely, the sacrifice on Calvary. The only other possibility is a sacrifice of thanksgiving. That the Lord's Supper cannot possibly be a sacrifice of propitiation follows from the unequivocal fact that, according to the New Testament, there is no work which works *ex opere operato*. The true sacrifice of praise is the proclamation of the gospel, faith, petition, prayer. The Lord's Supper can "be used" as such a sacrifice of praise or thanksgiving by the conscience, freed from fear, "making use" of ceremony *ad laudem Dei* [to the praise of God].

It is clear, as has been said, that Melanchthon, when speaking of the mass as a work, is motivated by the same interest as Luther. The viewpoint from which the action of the Lord's Supper is seen, is expressed in the question: What should the right attitude of the person be when receiving the Lord's Supper? The persistent tendency is to reject any idea of *ex opere operato*.

For our interconfessional conversation Melanchthon's way of stating the problem has been fateful, and for more than one reason. First of all, because the Catholic standpoint hardly has been given full justice; at any rate, it would be very unjust to repeat this polemic today, and use it upon all areas in which the theology of the sacrifice of the mass confronts us today in the Catholic Church. The Catholic understanding of Christ as the *principalis offerens* [the chief person offering] was not taken into consideration in this connection by Melanchthon. However this term is to be understood, in any case it is necessary to come to terms with it. Furthermore, it must be said that, also in Catholic circles, no one maintains that the liturgical act as such has the power of propitiation. The efficacy of the sacrifice of the mass has its basis in the fact that the sacrifice is Christ's own sacrifice. As the sacrifice of the church—and here the liturgical aspect may be brought in—the sacrifice of the mass works *quasi ex opere operato* [*i.e.*, by the mere completion of the act], and as the sacrifice of the celebrating priest and of those who co-sacrifice it works *ex opere operantis*, that is, *secundum dispositionem offerentium* [by the act of the one doing it, that is, according to the spiritual condition of those offering the sacrifice].

Above all, it must be emphasized that Melanchthon, in concentrating exclusively on the action in the Lord's Supper and its use by the Christian, did not penetrate to the real and deepest concern of the Catholic theology of the sacrifice of the mass. Bellarmine has showed this convincingly. He points out that Melanchthon does not get at the real center of the point in question. Melanchthon, he declares, overlooks that *sacrificium* is not only an *act*, but that in order that there shall be a sacrifice, there also needs to be an offering, *something to be sacrificed. In omni sacrificio proprie dicto requiritur res aliqua sensibilis, quae offertur, nec in sola actione sacrificium consistere potest.* [In every sacrifice, properly speaking, a certain visible thing to be offered is required, for sacrifice cannot consist in mere action.] As authority, he points, among other things, to Gen. 22:7, *Ecce ignis et ligna, ubi est victima holocausti?* ["Behold, the fire and the wood, but where is the victim for a burnt offering?"]

That this objection from Catholic thought is thoroughly to the point, can hardly be doubted without, at the same time, stress being placed upon the offering, the Host. In this connection we need only think of the well-known passage from the canons of the Council of Trent, session XXII, 2. There the identity of the sacrifice of Calvary and that of the mass is spoken of in these words: *Una enim eademque est hostia, idem nunc offerens sacerdotum ministerio, qui se ipsum tunc in cruce obtulit, sola offerendi ratione diversa.* [For there is one and the same victim, now offering through the ministry of priests, who then offered himself upon the cross, the only difference being in the means of being offered.] The identity of the sacrifice of Calvary with the sacrifice of the mass is twofold. The offering itself is the same, the body and blood of Christ being presented to God as a sacrifice in each case. And the sacrificing priest is the same, in so far as Christ is the *principalis offerens*. The act of sacrifice, on the other hand, is different. (The attempt of individual theologians belonging to the liturgical movement to show an identity in the act of sacrifice as well, and thus substantiate a threefold identity, seems not to have found very general recognition among Catholic theologians.) The identity of the sacrifice of Calvary and that of the mass consists, above all, in the offering, *illa munda oblatio* [that pure oblation], being the same. So the distinction is made in Catholic theology between *sacramentum* and *sacrificium* in view of the use of the elements: *Rationem sacrificii habet, inquantum offeretur; rationem autem sacramenti, inquantum sumitur.* [It has the meaning of sacrifice in so far as it is offered; and the meaning of sacrament in so far as it is received.][2]

It is striking that Bellarmine begins from the sacramental order or—if one so desires—from the *essence* of the Sacrament, whereas Melanchthon only speaks of the liturgical *action* and the *use* of the Sacrament. Bellarmine puts the question whether the body and blood of Christ can also be considered a host [*i.e.*, a victim], and whether the Eucharist is merely a sacrament or whether it can also be considered a sacrifice. Melanchthon, on the other hand, raises the question of the character of the action in the Lord's Supper. The question of the Lord's Supper and sacrifice has not been stated correctly until we clarify this relationship. All too often Protestants speak of the Lord's Supper and sacrifice, presentation and oblation, without really making clear whether one is speaking about a relationship that belongs to the essence of the Sacrament, or whether one is disregarding a sacramental relationship and is speaking about the "use" of the Sacrament.

However, Bellarmine shows that Luther—in contrast to Melanchthon—took this point into consideration, an investigation of which ought to be urgently considered. We thus can go on to Luther's chief objection against the sacrifice of the mass, namely, that it had been made into a sacrifice.

It is apparent that Luther is no longer speaking of one's attitude in communing or only of the "use" of the Sacrament. He is much more concerned with the Sacrament as such. He focused on the real center of the theology of the sacrifice of the mass. Of course, we cannot go into detail in this point any more than in the other sections of our presentation. However, it must be pointed out that Luther viewed sacrifice and communion as antagonistic concepts. That which is sacrificed to God cannot be received by us, and *vice versa.* Above all, Christ's words of institution show that the body and blood of Christ are offered in the Lord's Supper to the disciples, but not to God. Luther rejects the thought of the sacrifice of the mass not only because the mass is thus made into a work of human piety, but also because the popish Mass makes the Sacrament, Christ's body and blood, to be ?
a Host.

The decisive question for Melanchthon was how far the sacrifice of the Lord's Supper was to be admitted as propitiation or as thanksgiving. At this point also Bellarmine directed a critical remark: the first question is not whether there is here a sacrifice of propitiation or a sacrifice of thanksgiving, but the first question is whether the

Sacrament is a sacrifice at all. *Alia est controversia prior, utrum vere, ac proprium sacrificum offeratur.* [There is another controversy which is prior to this: whether it is true that a proper sacrifice is offered.][3]

Characteristically, Luther also does not think of the first question as being whether or not one should speak of a sacrifice of propitiation or of thanksgiving in regard to the Lord's Supper. His intention is to show that the Sacrament is no sacrifice at all. This is clearly shown from his *Exhortation on the Sacrament* of 1530. The historical background of this writing is, as is well known, the union negotiations which took place at this time. It shows that Luther knew of the compromise proposal of the Catholics according to which the Lord's Supper was to be called a *sacrificium memoriale.* There was to be no mention of it as a sacrifice of propitiation. But even if the Lord's Supper is allowed to be called a *sacrificium memoriale* instead of a sacrificium propitiatorium it is still being thought of as a sacrifice. That means that in the hand and mouth of the layman the Sacrament is merely a sacrament, but in the hand and mouth of the priest it is a sacrifice. For Luther the Sacrament itself is no sacrifice.[4] But the reception and "use" of the Sacrament can be designated as a sacrifice, a sacrifice of praise.

Thus we have touched the real problem. For the relationship of the Sacrament—or the Real Presence—and sacrifice is the problematical point. In our present theological situation this problem resolves itself again into a series of individual problems which should be mentioned briefly.

Modern Catholic theologians, especially those who belong to the liturgical movement, are seeking to understand this sacramental reality from the point of view of their *"Mysterientheologie."* The word "mystery" should not be taken intellectually. According to Odo Casel the word means specifically *not* a "doctrine," but a cultic mystic experience of the Divine.[5] It signifies the liturgical act through which the historical "act of salvation" is "made present." The mystery, in its sacramental character, is neither bound to the limits of time nor of space. It is the task of the Sacrament to preserve the *act* of redemption that happened in history as a continuing reality in the church. Not only applied grace, but the *act of redemption itself* is thus present. The Sacrament "brings back the past, it is the voice of the present, it reveals the future."[6] Protestant theologians have paid a certain amount of attention to this idea, the reason in some cases probably being that the expressions of this school concerning the *"representatio"* were thought to be in contrast to the usual Catholic teaching about the sacrifice of the mass as a "repetition" of the sacrifice of Christ. Nevertheless, this is a misunderstanding in every respect. Even within the Protestant fold similar thoughts are becoming noticeable. In connection with the Lord's Supper it is often said that Christ's *act of sacrifice* "is made present." In this view, it is said, lies the possibility of a connecting link to the idea of sacrifice in the Lord's Supper.

It is not our intention to enter upon the many complicated questions connected with *Mysterientheologie* and the presence of Christ's act of sacrifice. Our question is simply whether it is possible to legitimize these or similar views on the basis of evangelical faith.

We must raise the following serious question: Can examination show that the idea of a presence of Christ's act of sacrifice finds clear support *in the New Testament?* Within Catholicism, evidently, one can draw upon parallels from the history of religion and thus begin to theorize on worship in general. The fundamental Catholic view of the relationship of nature and grace allows that type of thinking: *Gratia non tollit naturam sed perficit.* [Grace does not abolish nature, but perfects it.] Of course, now and then there has arisen, also among Catholics, resistance to this idea. At any rate, the evangelical church cannot use such a method, except if its use can be defended with clear statements from the New Testament. Certainly statements can be found in the New Testament concerning the Lord's Supper as an eschatological event, in so far as the Lord's Supper is an anticipation of communion with Christ and the saints in that perfected kingdom of God. In chapter 5 of Revelation we meet the idea that Christ's sacrifice is eternally present before God in heaven. But to conclude from this that evidence has been furnished for connecting this statement with the idea that Christ's act of sacrifice is present in the sacramental act of worship, appears to be more than doubtful.

In addition, the question ought to be raised: Can the idea of a presence *in mysterio* of Christ's act of sacrifice be harmonized with the New Testament teaching of Christ's vicarious sacrifice? These reflections are meant to give new life to the antithesis of the Reformation. Catholic consciousness can cling without difficulty to the idea of a "bloodless" sacrifice of Christ or of His act of sacrifice being present today. However, for Luther the thought of a bloodless sacrifice was unacceptable and he undoubtedly would have passed the same judgment on the idea of a presence of the sacrifice of Christ. The contrast is rooted in the difference in the understanding of the atonement. According to Catholic understanding "sacrifice" has, primarily, an active meaning. Sacrifice is something which is presented to God *ad eum placendum* [in order to please Him].⁷ It is just as clear, on the other hand, that for Luther Christ's sacrifice is primarily, if not exclusively, something passive. To be sacrificed means to suffer death. The atonement, which is viewed by Catholics in the light of merit, is for Luther the vicarious suffering of punishment under the wrath of God. In a way totally different from the Catholics, Luther lays stress on the once-for-all valid event of the atonement, on the fact that the atonement *consummatum est.* ["It is finished."] What is to be sacrificed must suffer death. That is why Luther accuses the Catholic mass of being a re-crucifixion of Jesus Christ. This reproach was a necessary consequence of his teaching on the atonement. If the sacrifice of Christ is identical with His suffering of death under the wrath of God, then He can neither be sacrificed, nor can He sacrifice himself here and now, for that would be to say that He were to die here and now, which is an impossibility. If we wish to speak about Christ's act of sacrifice being present in and with the celebration of the Sacrament, we should first of all be certain that such an expression is possible without putting into question the "uniqueness" of the atonement wrought through Christ.

Another series of problems is connected with the understanding of Christ as *principalis agens* [the chief person acting] and our offering of ourselves during the Eucharist. Evangelical analysis also has been concerned with some of these ideas. Indeed in our study of this point we have drawn considerably closer to the Catholic position. For here also it is the question of the Sacrament as such and not only of a liturgical act. Those ideas which describe a unity of the believer with Christ in the eucharistic sacrifice play a large rôle in modern Catholicism, as we know. Christ is the *principalis offerens* of the sacrifice of the mass. The question is asked: To what extent can it be said of Christ that He sacrifices not only *virtualiter* but also *actualiter?* [not only virtually but also actually]. In other words, the question is whether Christ "makes a new act of sacrifice" with each new mass. The latter is accepted by some of the theologians who honor, in one form or another, the theory of oblation. Apart from them, however, there is by no means general agreement. But in any case, a connection is accepted between the sacrifice of the mass, whose metaphysical character is explained from the double consecration, and Christ as the eternally active high priest in heaven. The faithful are drawn into this sacrifice of Christ. The life of the church consists in co-acting with Christ. It lives and acts together with Him who is its head.

This acting reaches its high point in the sacrifice of the mass, through which the church outwardly offers the eucharistic sacrifice, and inwardly surrenders itself in the act of sacrificing. Thus Christ's sacrifice becomes the church's sacrifice. "He has committed His sacrifice to her in order that she present it as her sacrifice."[8] Similar ways of thinking have recently manifested themselves outside the Roman Church, too. We are confronted here by an attempt to identify a connection between our sacrifice and a special sacramental relationship. This attempt deserves our attention. Reference is made not just to our "intention to sacrifice" *during* the action of the Lord's Supper, but beyond that, of a connection of this intention to the sacramental event as such.

It was hoped to find support for such a view from Luther, and the well-known passage in his *Treatise on the New Testament* is readily quoted: "To be sure, this sacrifice of prayer, praise and thanksgiving, and of ourselves, we are not to present before God in our own person, but we are to lay it on Christ and let Him present it, as St. Paul teaches in Hebrews 13: 'Let us offer the sacrifice of praise to God continually, that is, the fruit of the lips which confess him and praise him,' and all this through Christ. For he is also a priest, as Psalm 110 says: 'Thou art a priest of ever after the order of Melchizedek'; because He intercedes for us in heaven, receives our prayer and sacrifice, and through Himself, as a godly priest, makes them pleasing to God, ..."[9]

Luther here clearly places the Lord's Supper, Christ's high-priestly work in heaven, and our offering of ourselves in association. The question is, however, what kind of association it is. In view of the train of thought which we have tried to follow in this presentation, the decisive problem arises whether this connection between the Lord's Supper, Christ's high-priestly work in heaven, and our offering of ourselves, belongs to the sacramental order as such; in other words, whether this connection, so to speak, takes effect through and with the consummation of the Sacrament, (the consecration; perhaps consecration and communion), or whether this connection is only of incidental character. If the former is true, then there is a connecting link between Luther and Catholic thought.

We cannot go into this question any more deeply at this point. However, it seems that there are those who—because of their interest in those expressions of Luther according to which the mass represents, in a certain sense, a sacrifice—are prepared to forget those much more powerfully emphasized expressions with which Luther wanted to show that the mass is *not* a sacrifice. First Luther wanted "Not that we offer the Sacrament, but that by our praise, prayer and sacrifice we move Him and give Him occasion to offer himself for us in heaven, and ourselves with Him."[10] It is not the Sacrament, not the body and blood of Christ, that is sacrificed, but simply our thanksgiving and praise. In addition Luther says that Christ's sacrifice takes place "without ceasing" and that our sacrifice should be offered "at all times," but at the same time it does not "necessarily and essentially" belong to the mass. Christ's sacrifice in heaven is, for Luther, nothing other than His continuous intercession, our sacrifice nothing other than the daily sacrifice of praise involved in dying unto self. This is the exercise of the universal priesthood, which takes place in such a way that "we may there come together and offer such sacrifice in common." Within Catholicism Christ's act of sacrifice in the mass is always viewed as something different from His general intercession, whereas in Luther such a distinction cannot be found. For Luther the eucharistic sacrifice has nothing to do with either the Real Presence or with the Sacrament. It is—to use a formulation with which Adolph Allwohn characterizes Luther's attitude toward worship—simply an individual occurrence of that which should always be there.[11]

Luther's understanding of worship cannot be decisive for us, however, but only the witness of the New Testament. We must limit ourselves again to but a few suggestions. The validity of the view with which we are concerned at present is dependent upon whether it can be established from the New Testament that in some way there is a connection between Christ's intercession and the Lord's Supper. Further, it is dependent upon whether there is another connection between the self-offering of the believer and the Lord's Supper, above and beyond that connection which exists simply in his consciousness. In addition, the validity of this view will be decided by the question whether, according to the New Testament, our self-offering can be seen to be connected with Christ's sacrifice, His sacrifice on Calvary with His intercession in heaven, or whether it is not much more the case that the sacrifice of Jesus Christ is unique, taking place in absolute loneliness. And finally, the validity of such a view depends decisively on whether the assumption that in and with a sacramental act a human self-offering takes place can be reconciled with the New Testament concept of faith. Against this assumption is the question, whether it is not an impossible assumption, simply because the New Testament understands faith to be a necessary part of sacrifice. At every one of these points one ought to come to grips with the exegesis of the Reformation.

A third group of problems concerns the relationship of communion and sacrifice. In Roman Catholicism the two usually are not treated together, especially because it is assumed of the priest that he offers sacrifice *in persona Christi* [representing Christ], whereas he communes *in propria persona* [in his own person]. However, we find this the more emphasized, then, in Anglican and occasionally also in more recent Lutheran theology, in which the attempt is made to show that the eucharistic meal is "the chief way in which to obtain a share in the sacrifice of Christ."[12] On the Anglican side the concept of sacrifice is used to maintain that sacrifice is in no way just the slaughter of the sacrificial lamb, but rather the sacrificial meal itself is part of the sacrifice.[13] On the Lutheran side this motive can—as has actually been done—be connected with a strong emphasis on the Real Presence. Thus it can be said that we receive in the Lord's Supper the same sacrifice which once was presented on Calvary. For in receiving here on earth the gift of the mercy of God in this unique way, namely in the body and blood of Jesus Christ, the sacrifice of thanksgiving can rise higher from no other place than from the place where the gift of grace is received.

This view is thoroughly plausible in its evangelical intention. Nevertheless, it is necessary to test the concept of a "sacrificial meal" with the New Testament. The meaning of this expression could lie in "partaking" of the sacrifice through communion. This is doubtless a New Testament thought. We partake through communion of the same body and blood that was given unto death. But we ought to be sure that the expression "sacrificial meal" is appropriate to describe this relationship. The expression appears much more to indicate that through the communion one actively "takes part" in the sacrifice. Many objections must be raised against this, however. For such a way of thinking would tend to obliterate the distinction between the *"factum passionis"* and the *"usus passionis,"* something which Luther has pointed out. That communion is an act of sacrifice is not indicated in any passage of the New Testament. The form of the verb ἐκχυννόμενον [to be shed] appears in the present, thus pointing to something that is going to happen *soon*. The expression, therefore, talks of Jesus' death on the cross and not that His blood is to be shed in the Lord's Supper, as Catholic theologians and, incidentally, Luther also, assumed. In 1 Cor. 10:18-21 the Lord's Supper is compared to the Jewish and pagan sacrificial meals, but the parallel is drawn no further than the participation in eating the sacrificial food. That communion means participation in the act of sacrifice finds mention nowhere. An important question is also whether the uniqueness of the sacrifice of Christ as a vicarious suffering of punishment must not raise questions concerning the connection of the Real Presence with the terminology of sacrifice. The body and blood which we receive *has been* presented to God as a sacrifice; *now* it is a gift received by us.

Our purpose with these remarks was to lay bare the relationship between the idea of sacrifice and the Sacrament or the Real Presence. That the use of the idea of sacrifice in connection with the action of the Lord's Supper can take place should without question be apparent without more ado, so long as the aspect of *thanksgiving* is maintained. It would even be desirable for this idea to find itself a place. The "service" character of our worship services ought to be more strongly emphasized, whereas the penitential attitude and, connected with it, the individualism of traditional Lutheran piety at the Lord's Supper, ought to be limited and corrected by an emphatic stress on the Lord's Supper as communion and eucharist. However, concerning the understanding of Christ's body and blood and its reception under the forms of bread and wine, Luther's distinction between the "Sacrament itself" and the "reception and use of the Sacrament" is thoroughly correct.

There is one thing that must be added to our presentation. A sacrifice of praise and thanksgiving has meaning only through the sacrifice of our own selves, that is, through giving our self up unto death. Perhaps one side of the "reception and use of the Sacrament" thus deserves to be stressed when it comes to talking of worship and sacrifice. The life of the Christian is a life under the sign of baptism. Through baptism our whole selfish self has been consecrated unto death. In baptism we have, as Luther says, stepped out into the Jordan. There, however, are the priests with the ark, whereas the waters begin to cover us. "The priests carry and uphold the ark in Jordan when [in the hour of our death or peril] they preach and administer to us this Sacrament . . . Baptism leads us into a new life on earth; the bread guides us through death into eternal life."[14]

We, not the Sacrament, are the sacrifice. But we live from the gifts of God's grace, that is, we are led through them from death to life. Sacrifice consists in just this.

This event finds expression in worship through thanksgiving, praise, creed, and witness. But a true sacrifice is only this when it is consecrated through faith by daily walking in baptism, that is, walking in fear and faith, death and resurrection.

At the end of our presentation perhaps a word of Gregory Dix might serve to give a bit of life to what has been said. "The ancient Church," says Dix, "trained the confessors as she had trained the martyrs—by the liturgy."[15] This expression points deeply into the essence of self-sacrifice: "Lo, I come. . . . I delight to do thy will, O my God" (Psalm 40: 7,8).

NOTES

[1] Robert Bellarmine, Latin Works, Paris: 1870-74, Tom. III, *De missa.* Liber. I, Cap. II.

[2] Thomas Aquinas, *Summa Theologiae,* III, 79, 5.

[3] Bellarmine, *op. cit.,* Cap. V.

[4] cf. Weimar edition of Luther's works (WA), XXXII, 612, 30.

[5] *Jahrbuch für Liturgiewissenschaft,* XV, p. 278.

[6] Anscar Vonier, "A Key to the Doctrine of the Eucharist," in *Collected Works,* II, 1952.

[7] Thomas Aquinas, *op. cit.,* III, 48, 3.

[8] G. L. Bauer, "Das heilige Messopfer im Lichte des heiligen Thomas," in *Divus Thomas,* 1950, p. 25.

[9] *Works of Martin Luther,* Phila. ed., I, p. 314; WA, VI, 368.

[10] *ibid.,* pp. 314 f.; WA, VI, 369.

[11] Adolph Allwohn, *Gottesdienst und Rechtfertigungsglaube,* Luthers Grundlegung evangelischer Liturgik bis zum Jahre 1523, Göttingen: 1926, p. 7.

[12] Rudolph Stählin, "Das Herrenmahl als Opfer," in *Evangelisch-Lutherische Kirchenzeitung,* 1949, pp. 263-266.

[13] C. N. Hicks, "The Eucharistic Sacrifice," in *Ways of Worship:* The Report of a Theological Commission of Faith and Order, London: SCM Press, 1951, p. 207.

[14] Luther, "A Treatise concerning the Blessed Sacrament of the Holy and True Body of Christ and concerning the Brotherhoods," 1519, Phila. ed., II, pp. 25 f.; WA, II, 753 f. (The phrase in brackets is omitted in the Weimar edition quoted by the author.)

[15] Dom Gregory Dix, *The Shape of the Liturgy,* London: Dacre Press, 1945, p. 394.

THE AUTHORS

DR. CONRAD BERGENDOFF, President of Augustana College, Rock Island, Illinois. Address: 835 35th Street, Rock Island, Illinois. U. S. A.

DR. PETER BRUNNER, Professor of Systematic Theology at the University of Heidelberg. Address: Hauptstrasse 242, Heidelberg, Germany.

DR. BO GIERTZ, Bishop of the Diocese of Gothenburg. Address: V. Hamngatan 17, Gothenburg C, Sweden.

DR. MARTIN J. HEINECKEN, Professor of Systematic Theology and Ethics at the Lutheran Theological Seminary. Address: 7301 Germantown Avenue, Philadelphia 18, Pennsylvania. U. S. A.

DR. T. A. KANTONEN, Professor of Systematic Theology at the Hamma Divinity School. Address: 954 Pythian Avenue, Springfield, Ohio. U. S. A.

DR. KARL KARNER, Professor of New Testament at the Evangelical Lutheran Academy of Budapest. Address: Csengery-u 64, Budapest VI, Hungary.

DR. ERNST KINDER, Professor of Dogmatics at the University of Münster. Address: Martin Luther Street 4, Münster, Westphalia, Germany.

DR. CHRISTHARD MAHRENHOLZ, Chairman of the Lutheran Liturgical Conference of Germany. Address: Kerstingstrasse 28, Hanover, Germany.

DR. ANDERS NYGREN, Bishop of the Diocese of Lund. Address: Lund, Sweden.

DR. REGIN PRENTER, Professor of Systematic Theology at the University of Aarhus. Address: Trøjborgvej 58, Aarhus, Denmark.

DR. VILMOS VAJTA, Director of the Department of Theology, Lutheran World Federation. Address: 17 Route de Malagnou, Geneva, Switzerland.

DR. CARL FR. WISLÖFF, Rector of the Practical-Theological Seminary, Free Theological Faculty. Address: Fastingsgate 4, Oslo, Norway.